ISBN 978-1-61780-552-3

HAL•LEONARD®
CORPORATION

7777 W. BLUEMOUND RD. P.O. BOX 13819 MILWAUKEE, WI 53213

Visit Hal Leonard Online at
www.halleonard.com

Awesome God

Registration 7
Rhythm: 16-Beat or Pop

Words and Music by
Rich Mullins

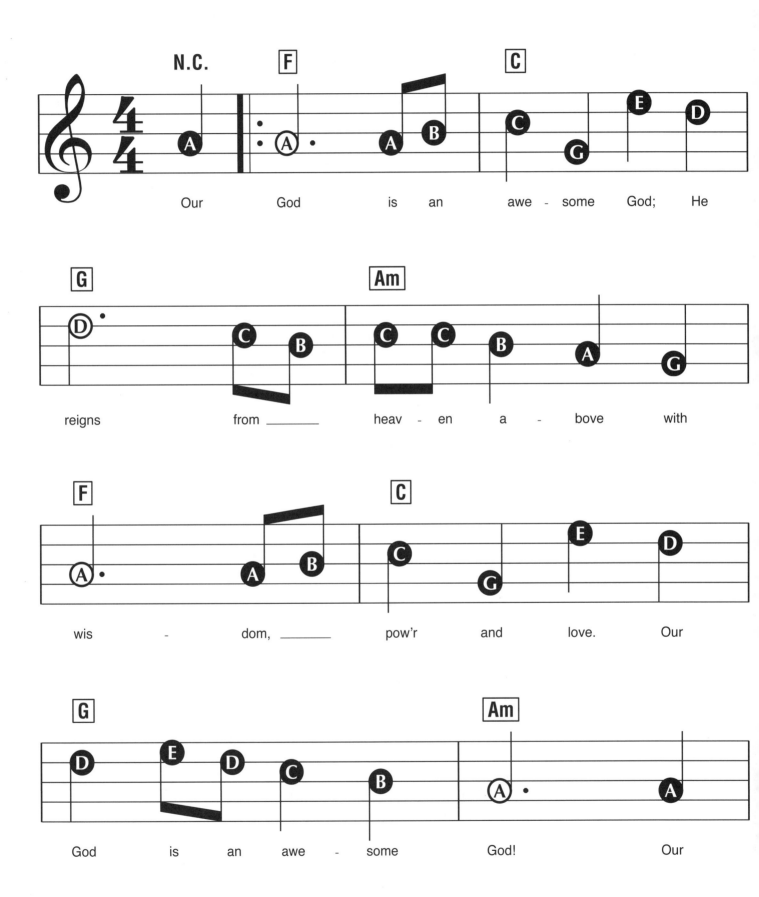

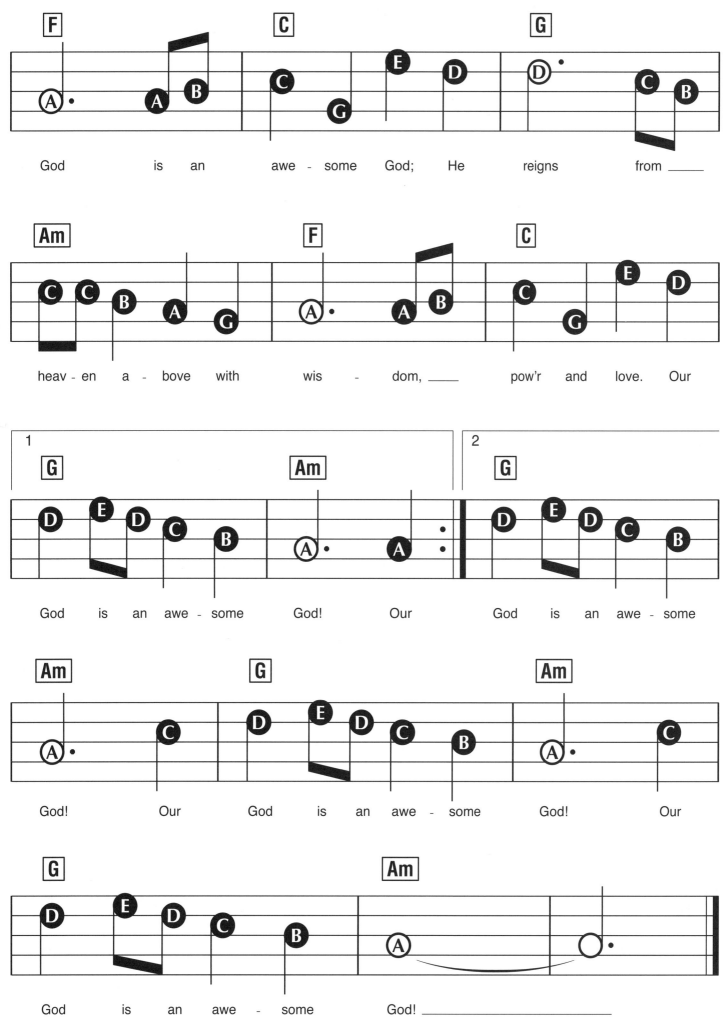

Better Is One Day

Registration 2
Rhythm: 8-Beat or Pop

Words and Music by
Matt Redman

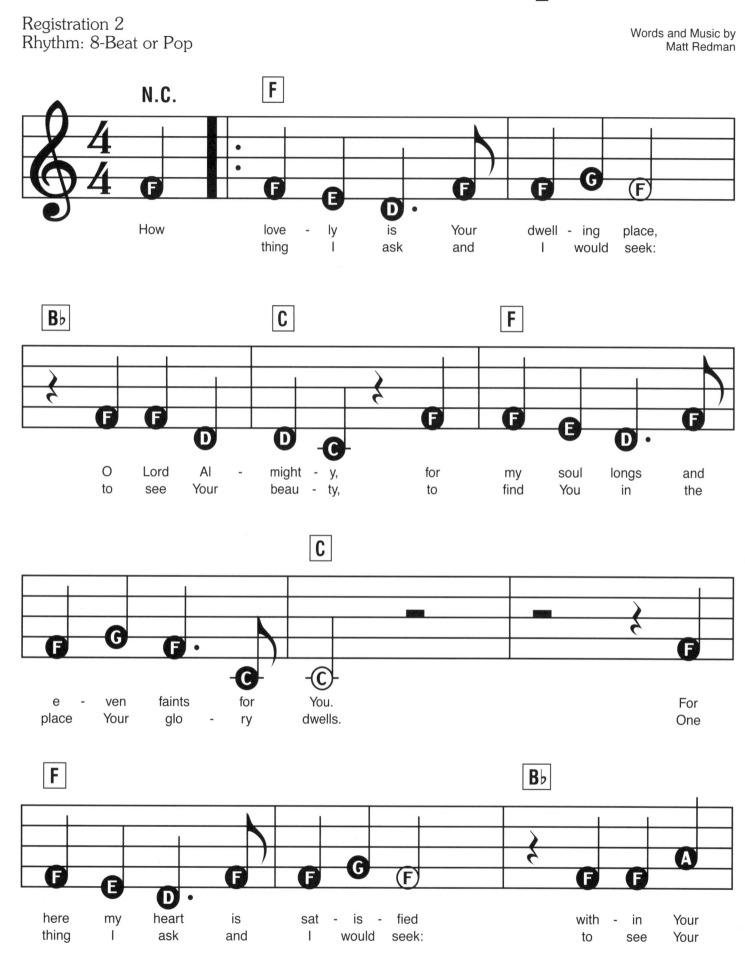

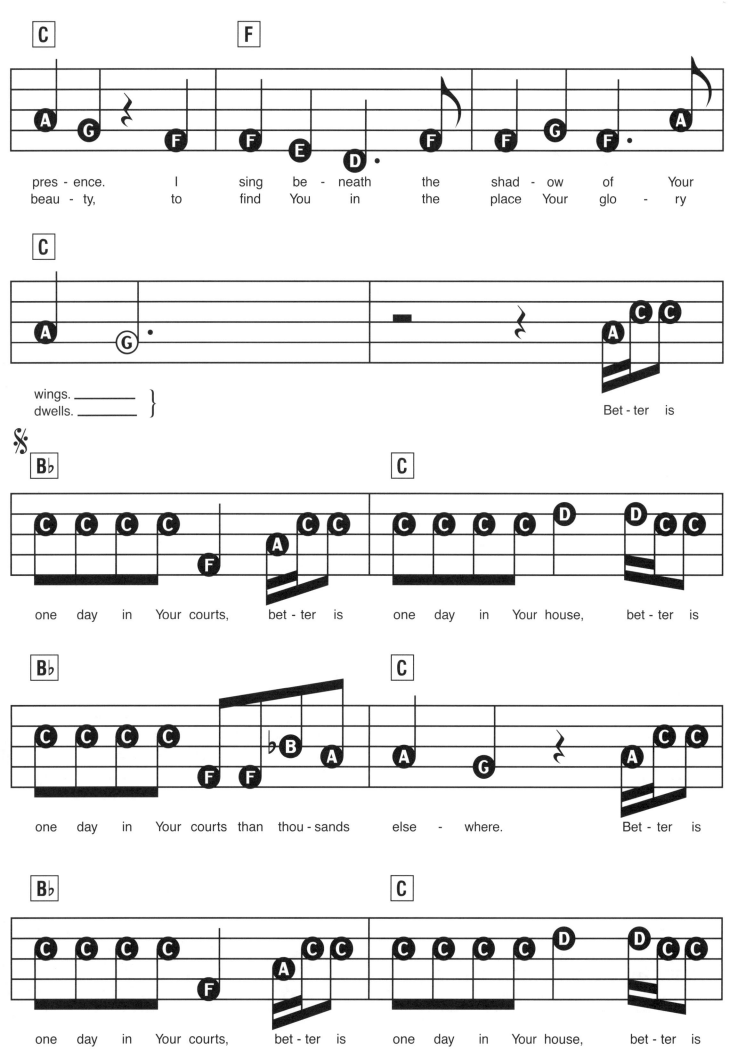

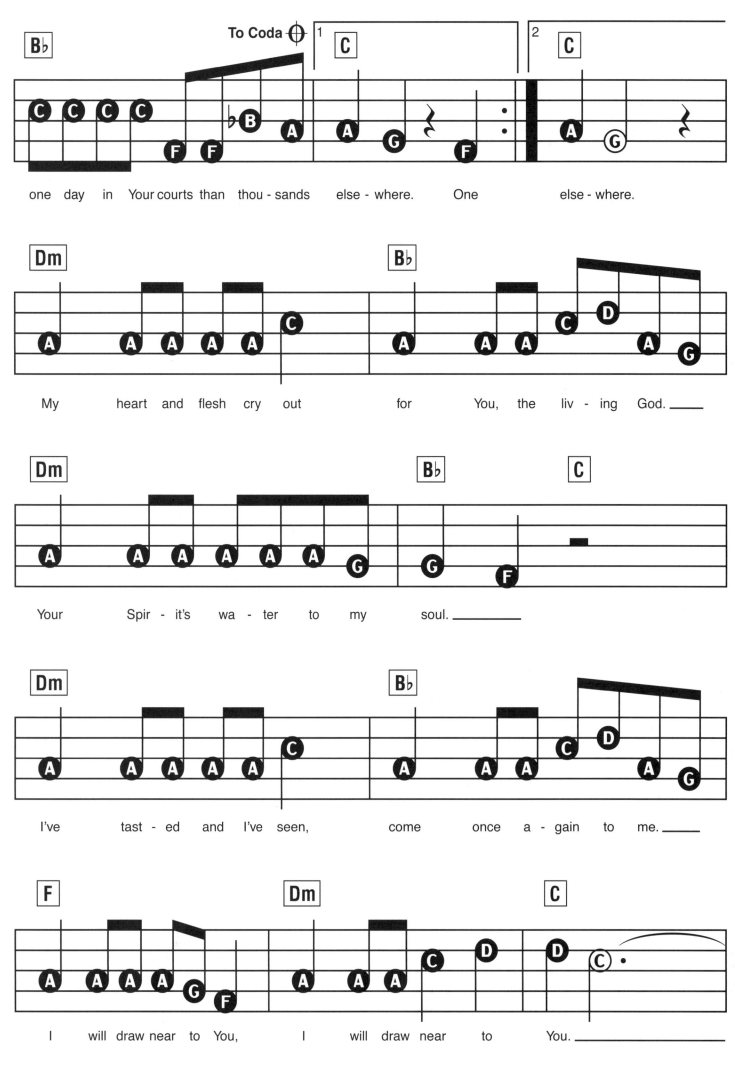

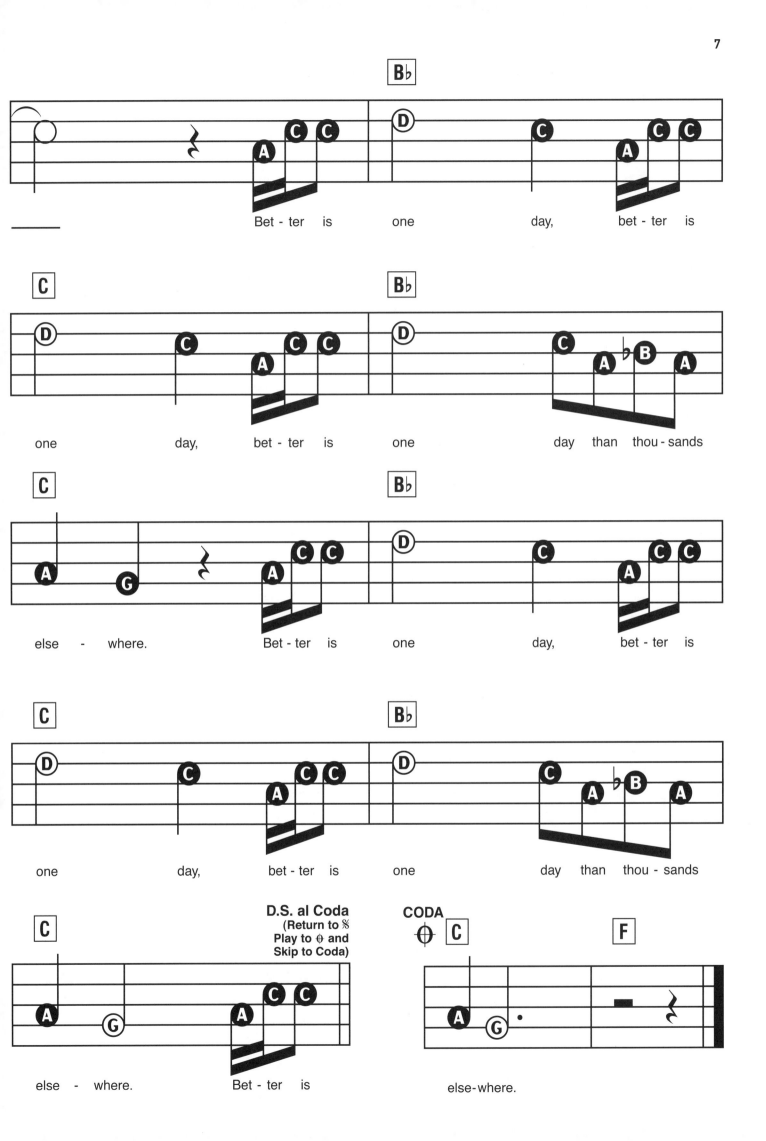

Blessed Be Your Name

Registration 4
Rhythm: 8-Beat or Rock

Words and Music by Matt Redman
and Beth Redman

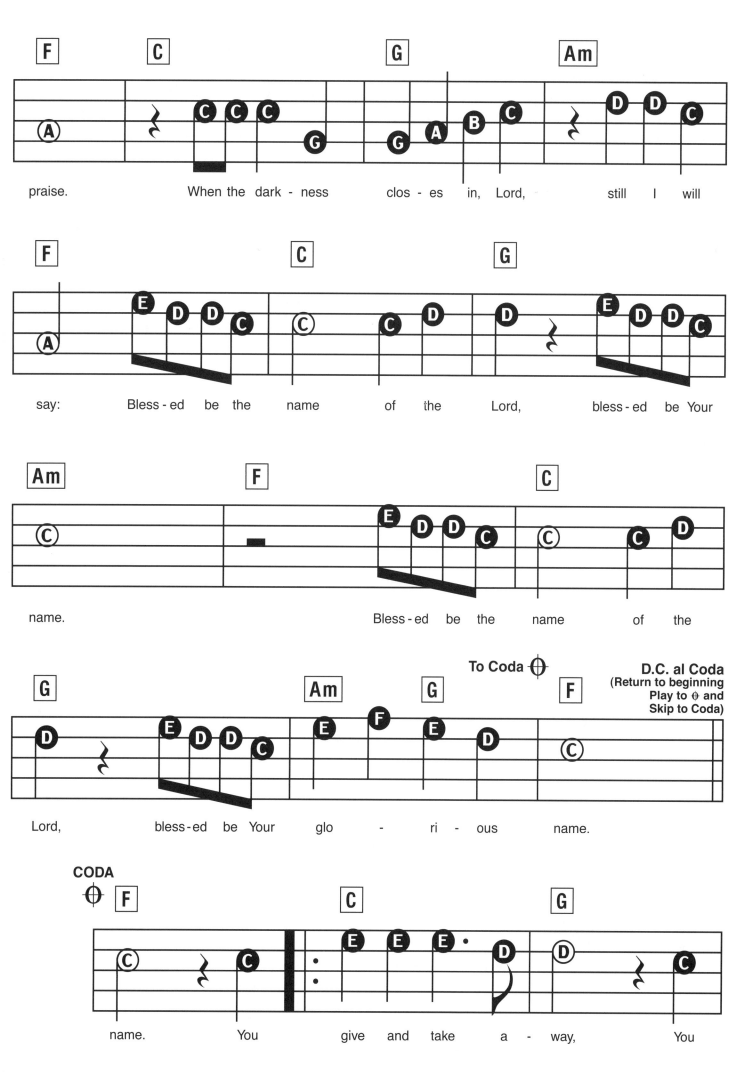

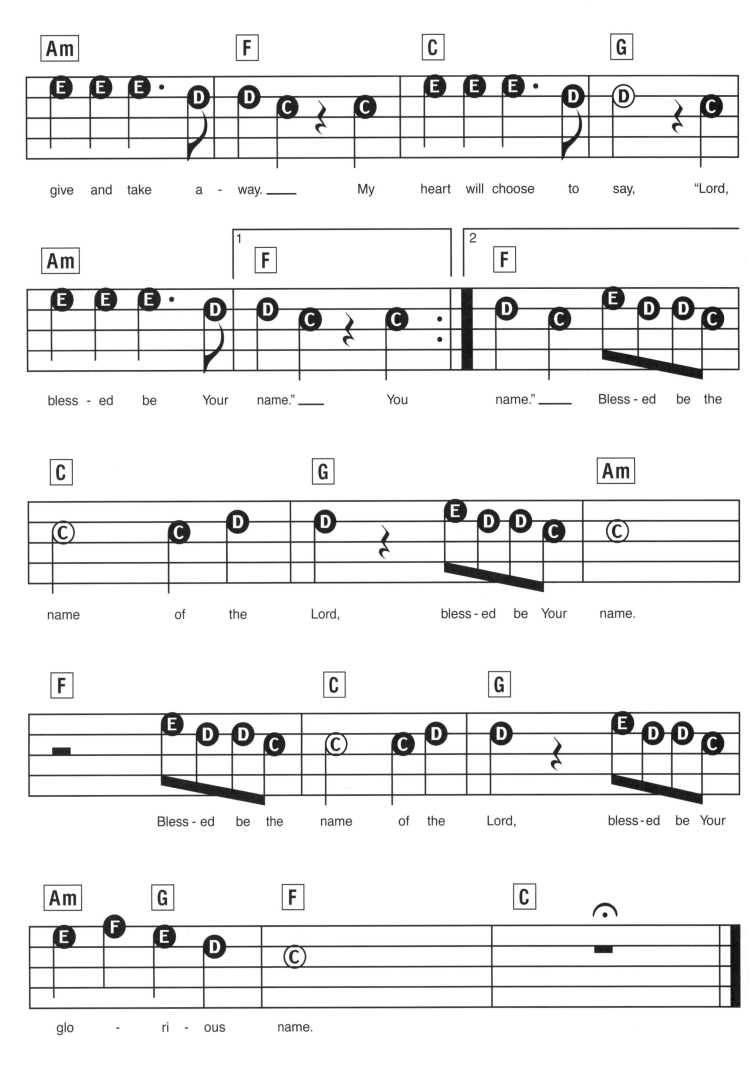

Give Us Clean Hands

Registration 1
Rhythm: Ballad or 8-Beat

Words and Music by
Charlie Hall

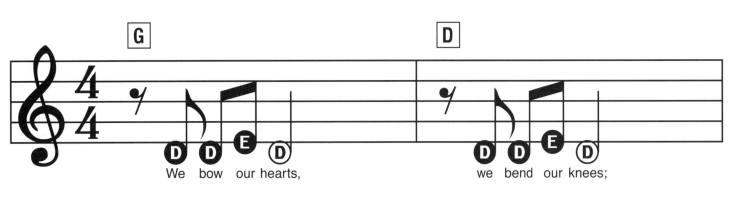

We bow our hearts,   we bend our knees;

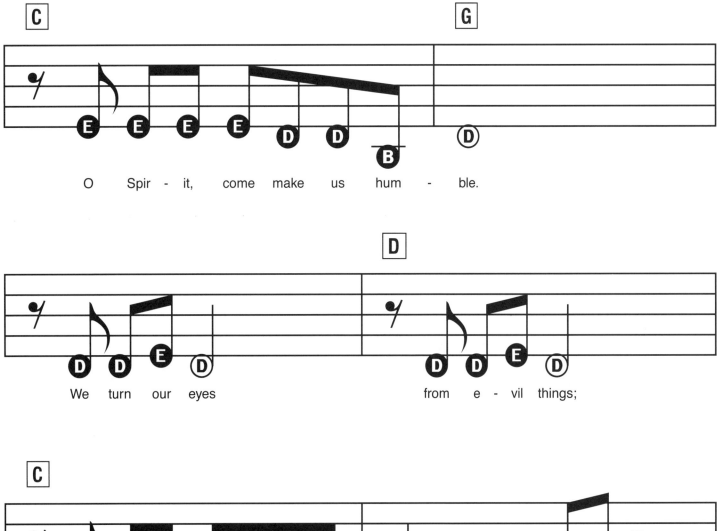

O Spir - it, come make us hum - ble.

We turn our eyes   from e - vil things;

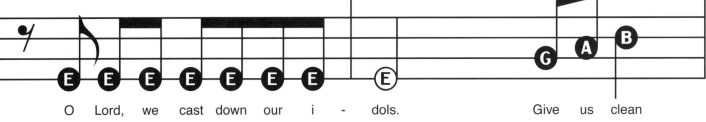

O Lord, we cast down our i - dols.   Give us clean

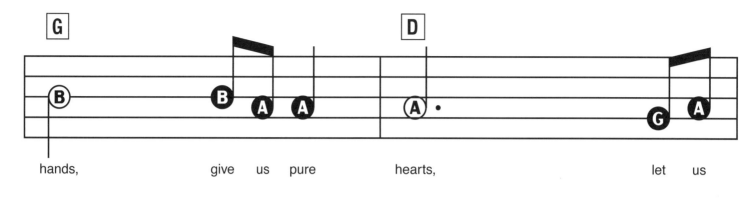

hands, give us pure hearts, let us

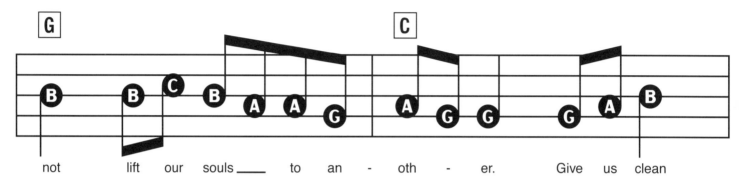

not lift our souls ___ to an - oth - er. Give us clean

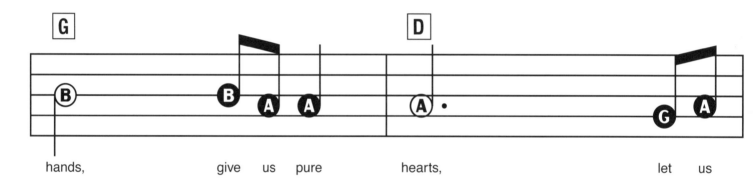

hands, give us pure hearts, let us

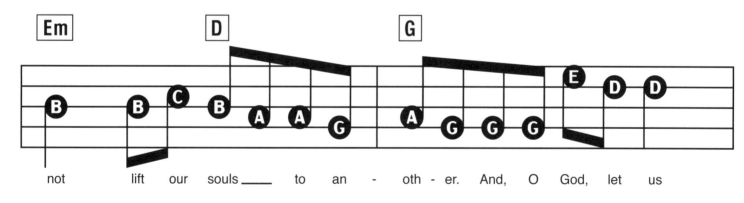

not lift our souls ___ to an - oth - er. And, O God, let us

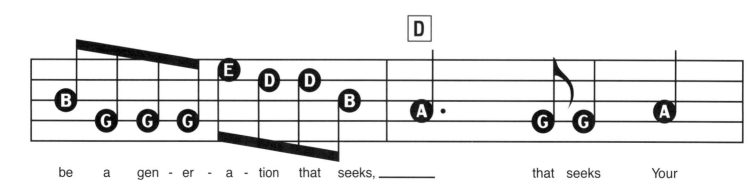

be a gen - er - a - tion that seeks, _____ that seeks Your

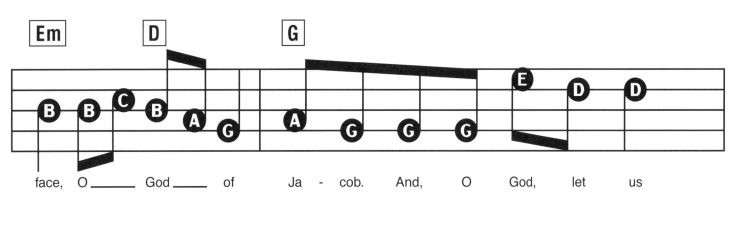

face, O ____ God ____ of Ja - cob. And, O God, let us

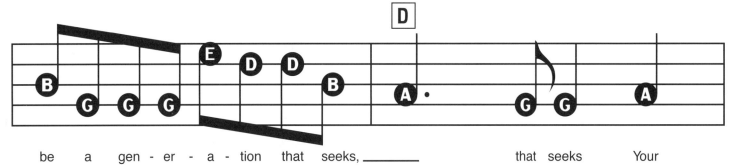

be a gen - er - a - tion that seeks, _____ that seeks Your

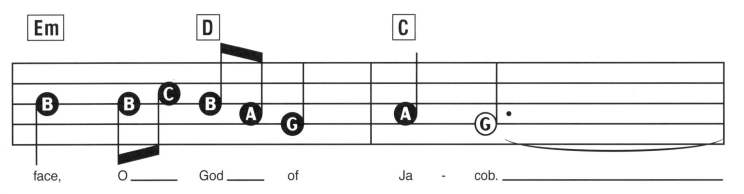

face, O ____ God ____ of Ja - cob. _____

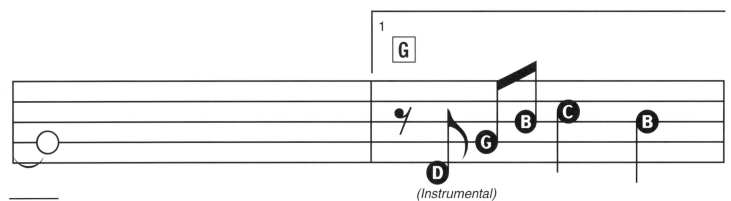

(Instrumental)

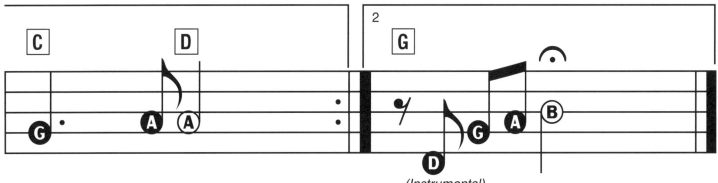

(Instrumental)

Breathe

Registration 1
Rhythm: Ballad or 8-Beat

Words and Music by
Marie Barnett

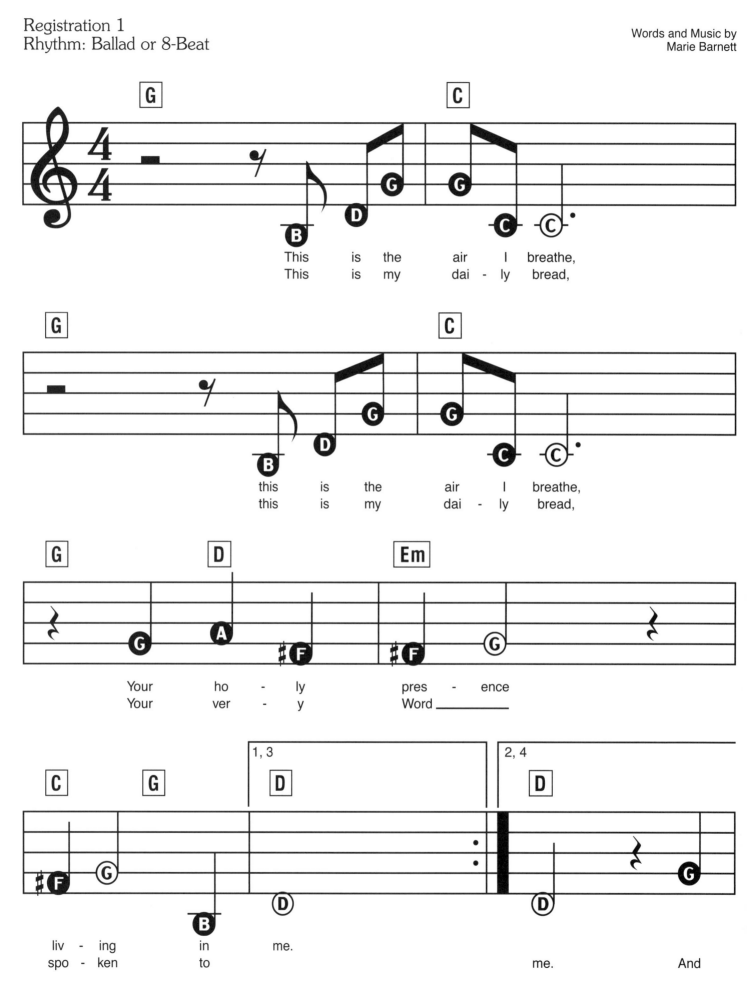

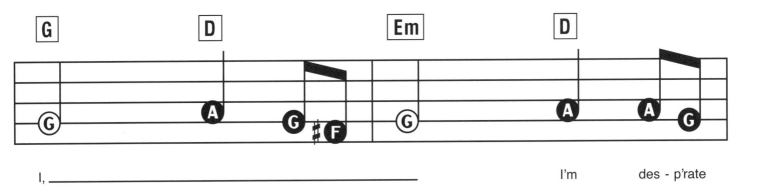

I, _____ I'm des - p'rate

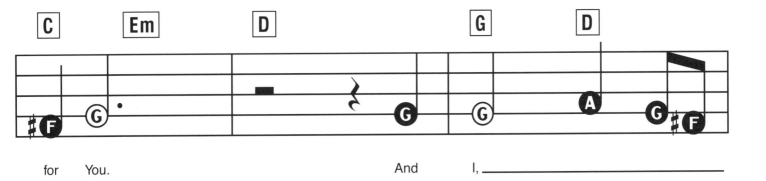

for You. And I, _____

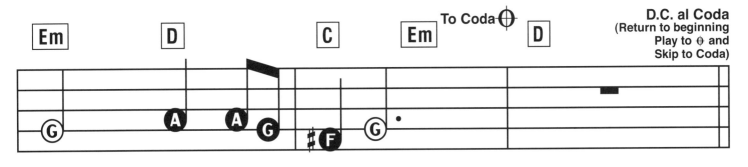

____ I'm lost with - out You.

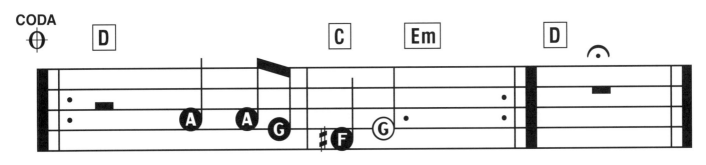

I'm lost with - out You.

Draw Me Close

Registration 1
Rhythm: Ballad or 8-Beat

Words and Music by
Kelly Carpenter

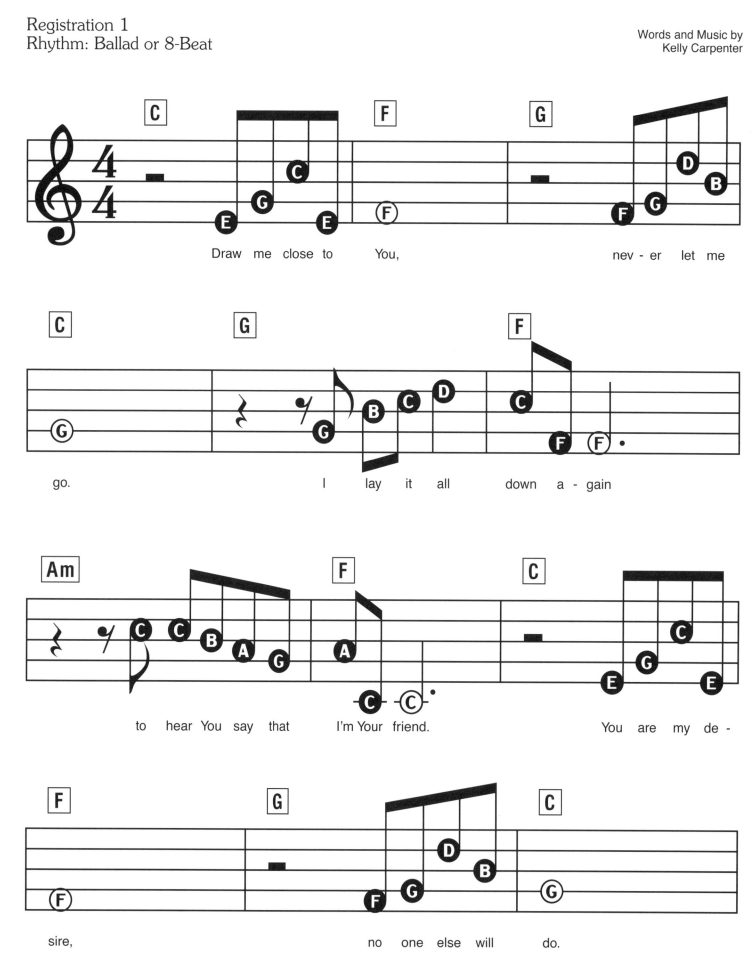

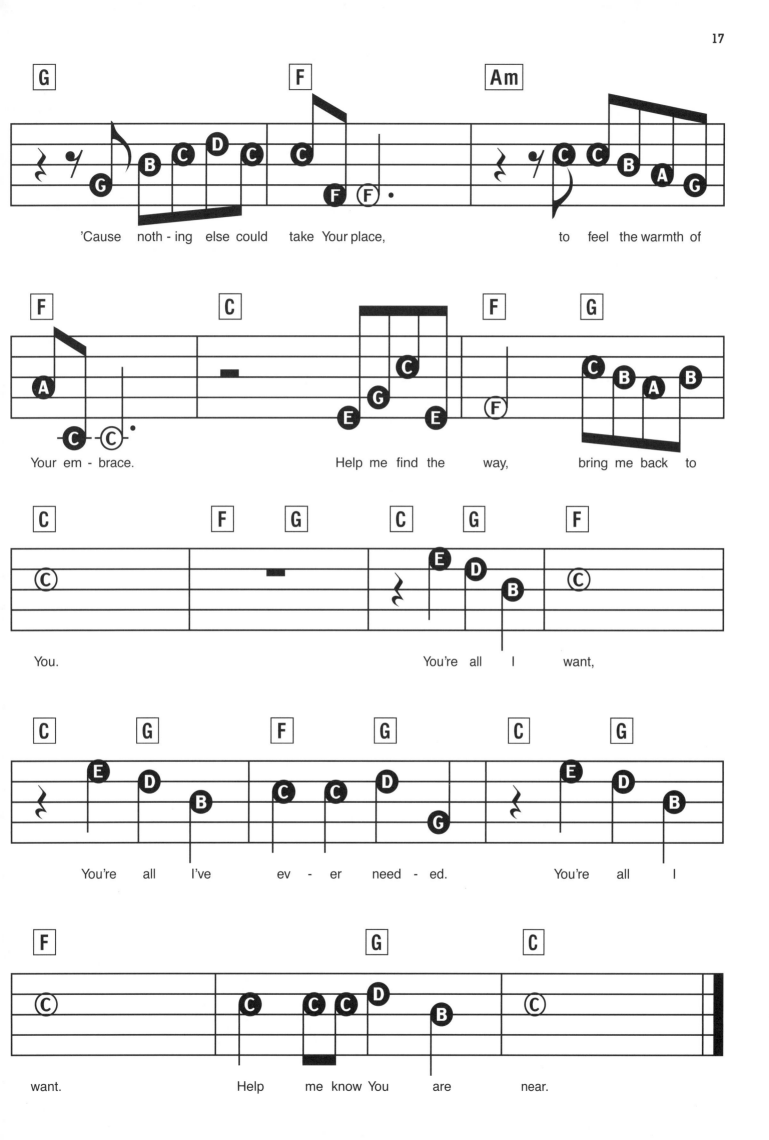

Everyday

Registration 8
Rhythm: 8-Beat or Rock

Words and Music by
Joel Houston

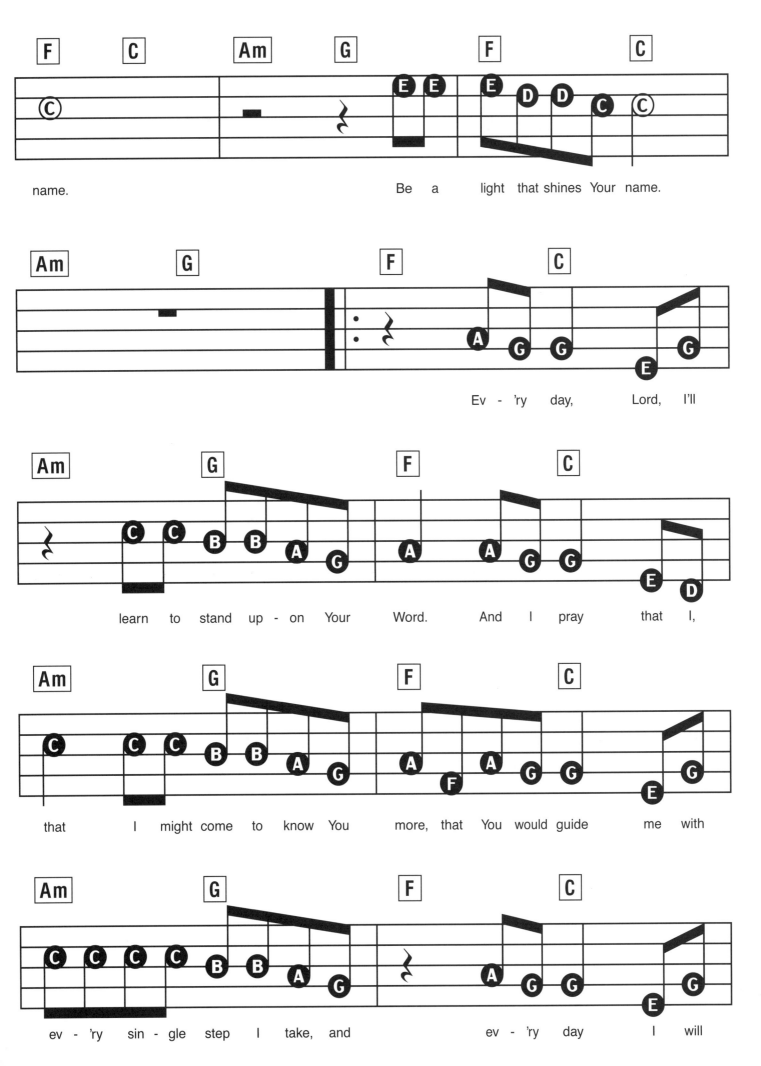

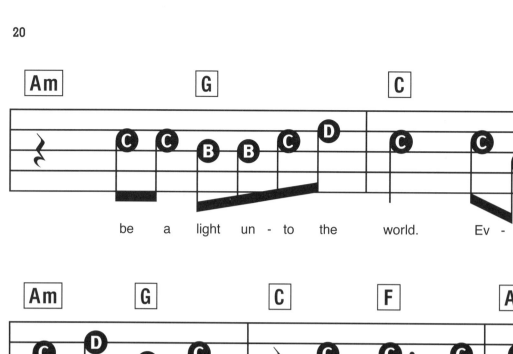

be a light un - to the world. Ev - 'ry day it's

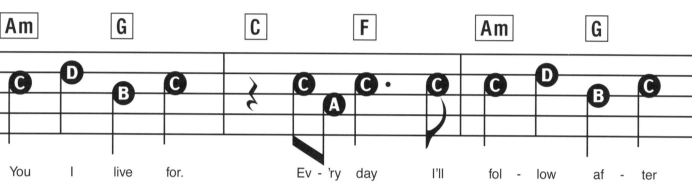

You I live for. Ev - 'ry day I'll fol - low af - ter

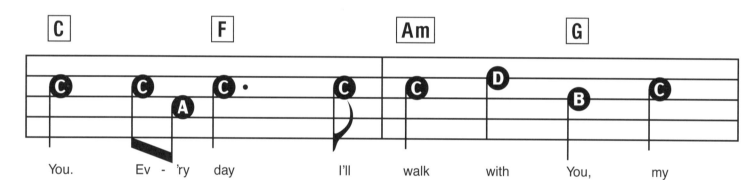

You. Ev - 'ry day I'll walk with You, my

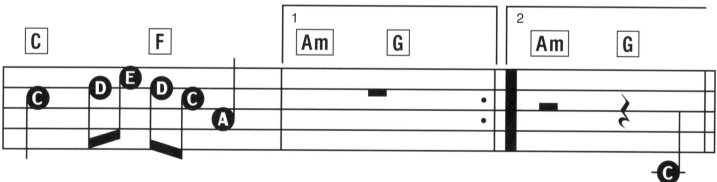

Lord. _____

It's

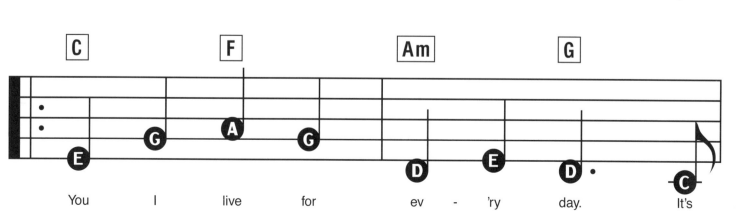

You I live for ev - 'ry day. It's

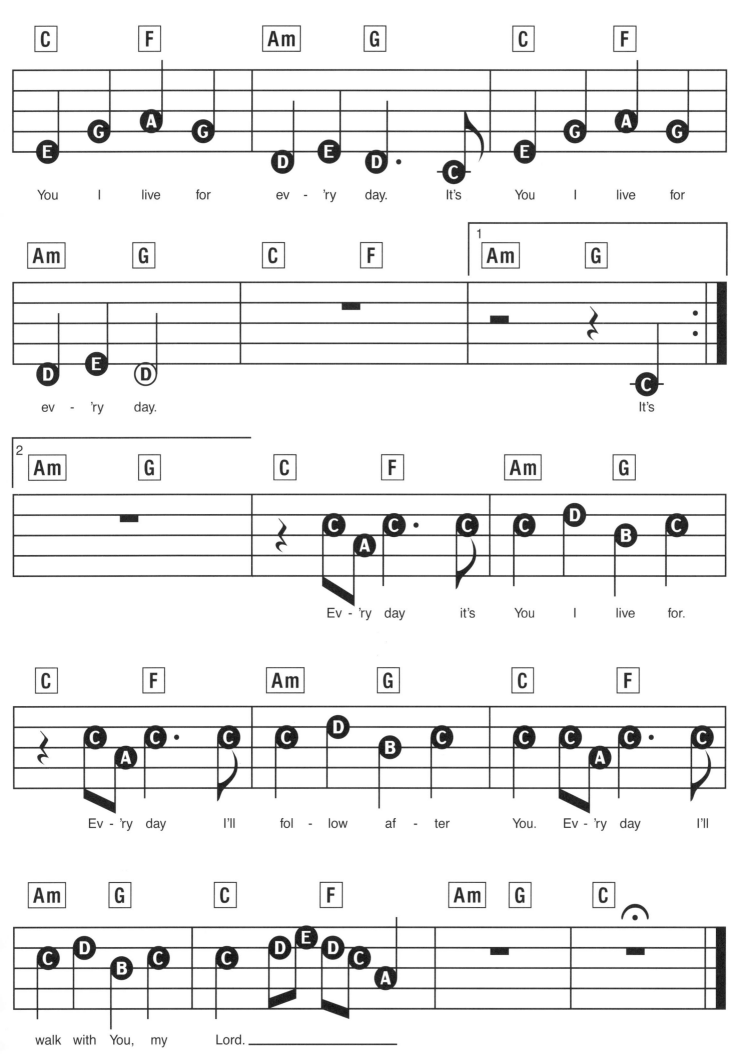

Forever

Registration 2
Rhythm: 8-Beat or Rock

Words and Music by
Chris Tomlin

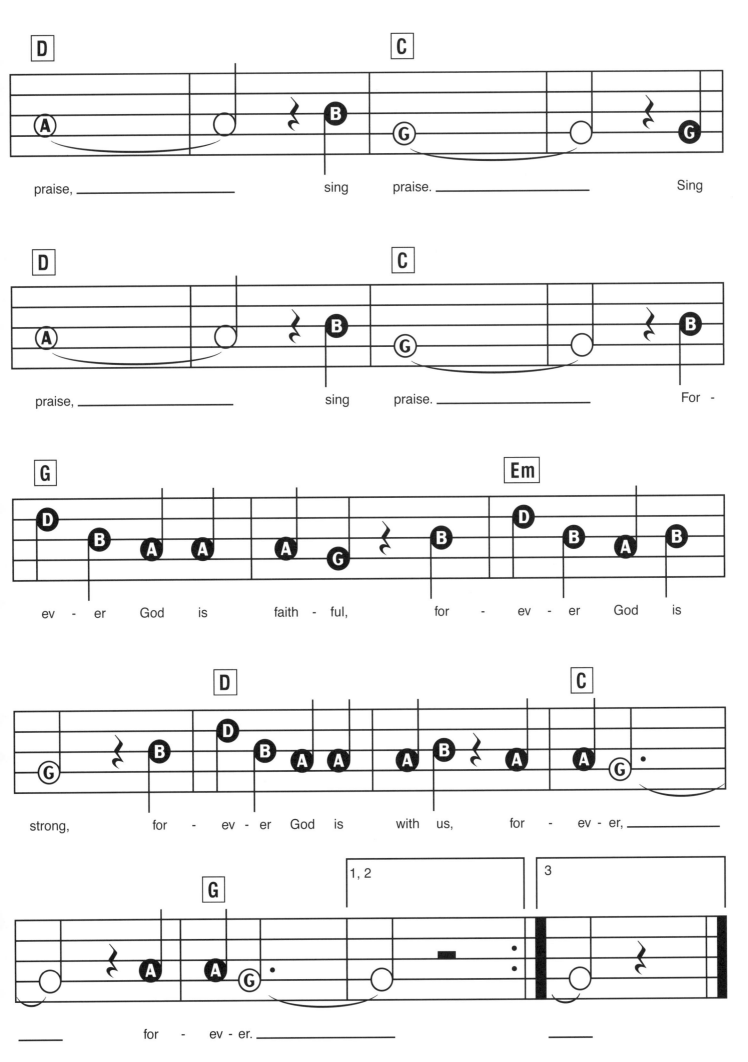

Grace Flows Down

Registration 3
Rhythm: Ballad

Words and Music by Louie Giglio,
David Bell and Rod Padgett

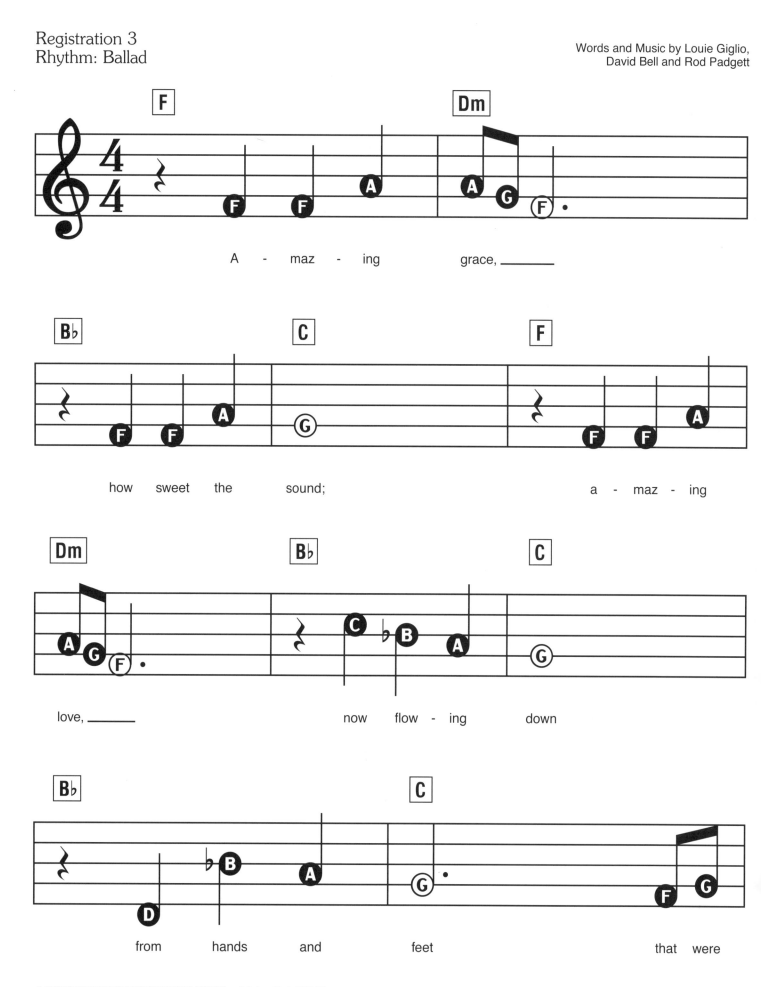

25

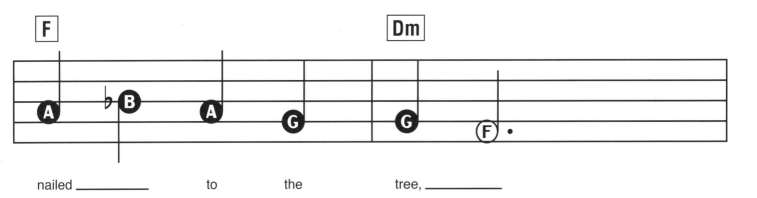

nailed _____ to the tree, _____

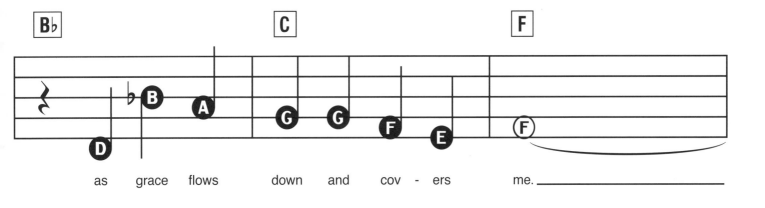

as grace flows down and cov - ers me. _____

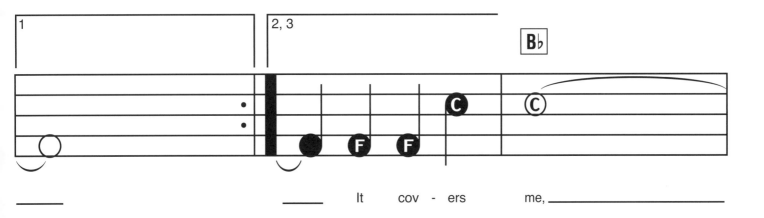

_____   _____ It cov - ers me, _____

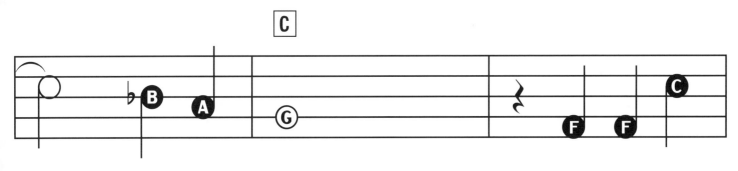

_____   it cov - ers

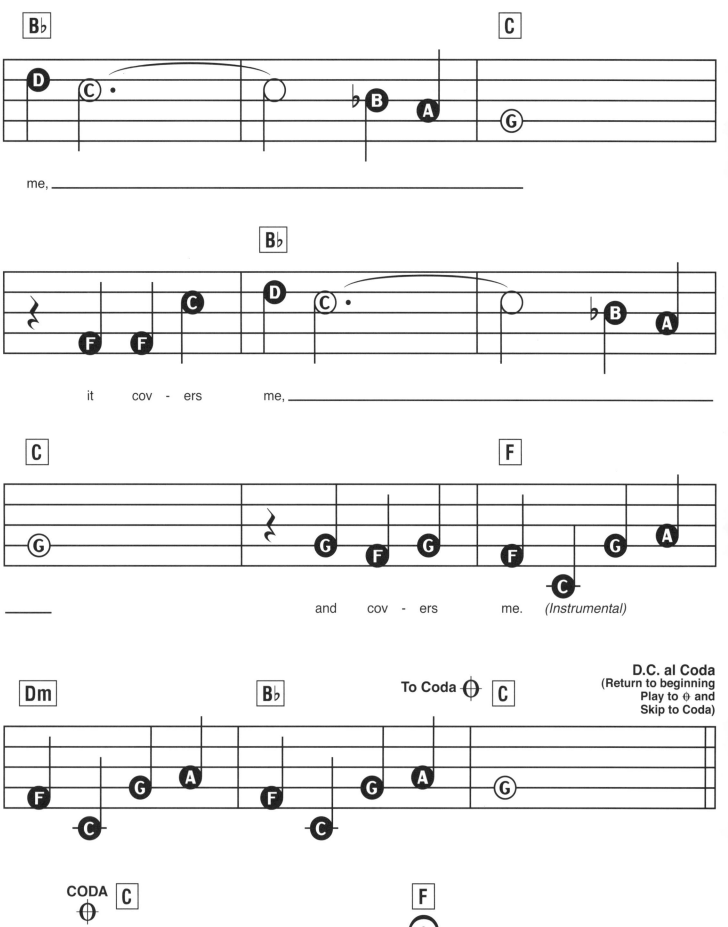

me, _____

it cov - ers me, _____

_____ and cov - ers me. *(Instrumental)*

D.C. al Coda
(Return to beginning
Play to ⊕ and
Skip to Coda)

To Coda ⊕

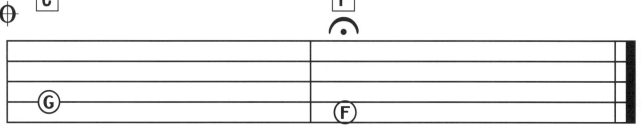

How Great Is Our God

Registration 4
Rhythm: 8-Beat or Ballad

Words and Music by Chris Tomlin,
Jesse Reeves and Ed Cash

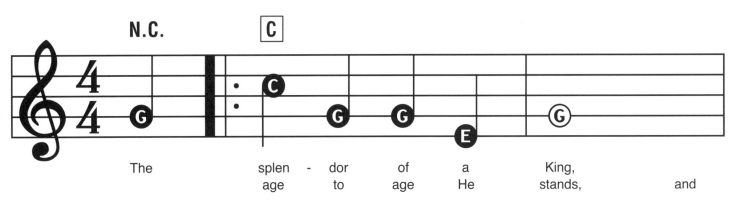

The splen - dor of a King,
age to age He stands, and

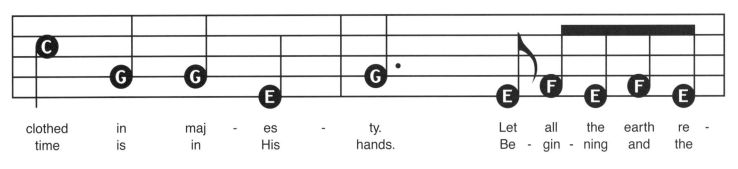

clothed in maj - es - ty. Let all the earth re -
time is in His hands. Be - gin - ning and the

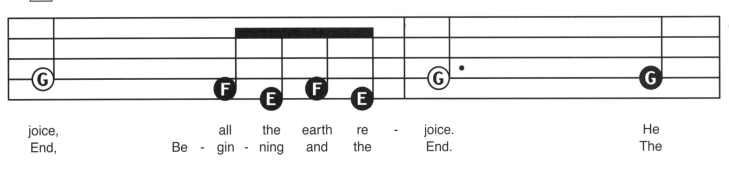

joice, all the earth re - joice. He
End, Be - gin - ning and the End. The

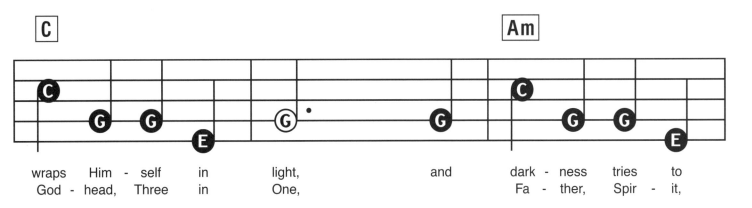

wraps Him - self in light, and dark - ness tries to
God - head, Three in One, Fa - ther, Spir - it,

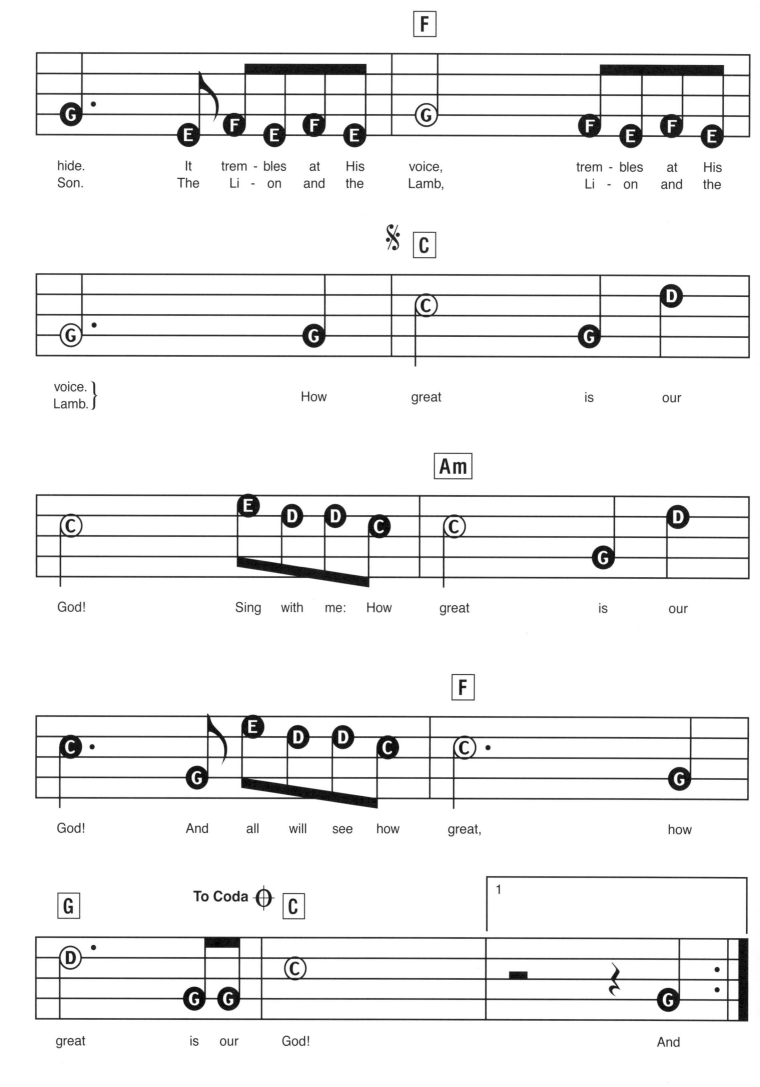

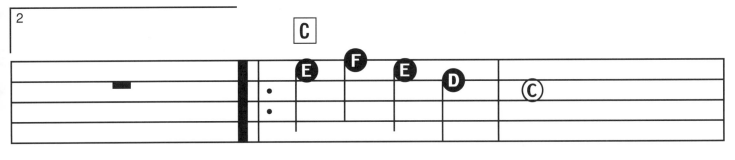

Name a - bove all names,

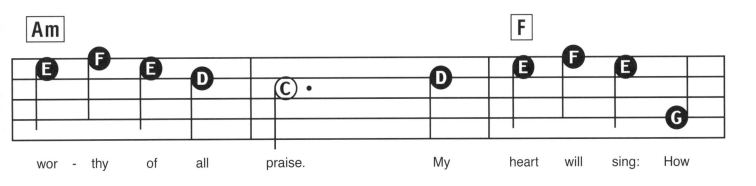

wor - thy of all praise. My heart will sing: How

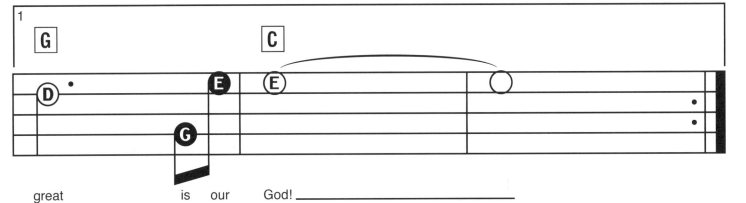

great is our God! _____

D.S. al Coda
(Return to %
Play to ⊕ and
Skip to Coda)

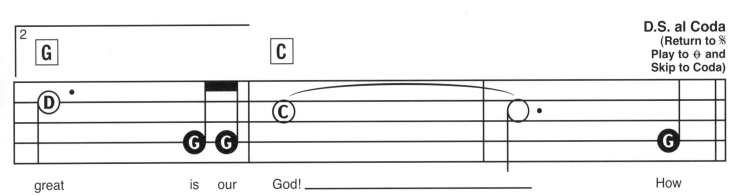

great is our God! _____ How

CODA
⊕ C

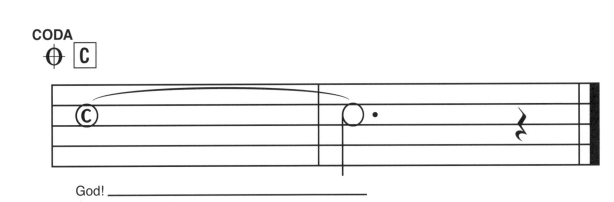

God! _____

Hosanna
(Praise Is Rising)

Registration 4
Rhythm: 8-Beat or Rock

Words and Music by Paul Baloche
and Brenton Brown

G

Praise _____ is ris - ing,
Hear _____ the sound _____ of

C

eyes _____ are turn - ing to You,
hearts _____ re - turn - ing to You,

G

we turn to You.
we turn to You.

Hope _____ is stir - ring,
In _____ Your King - dom

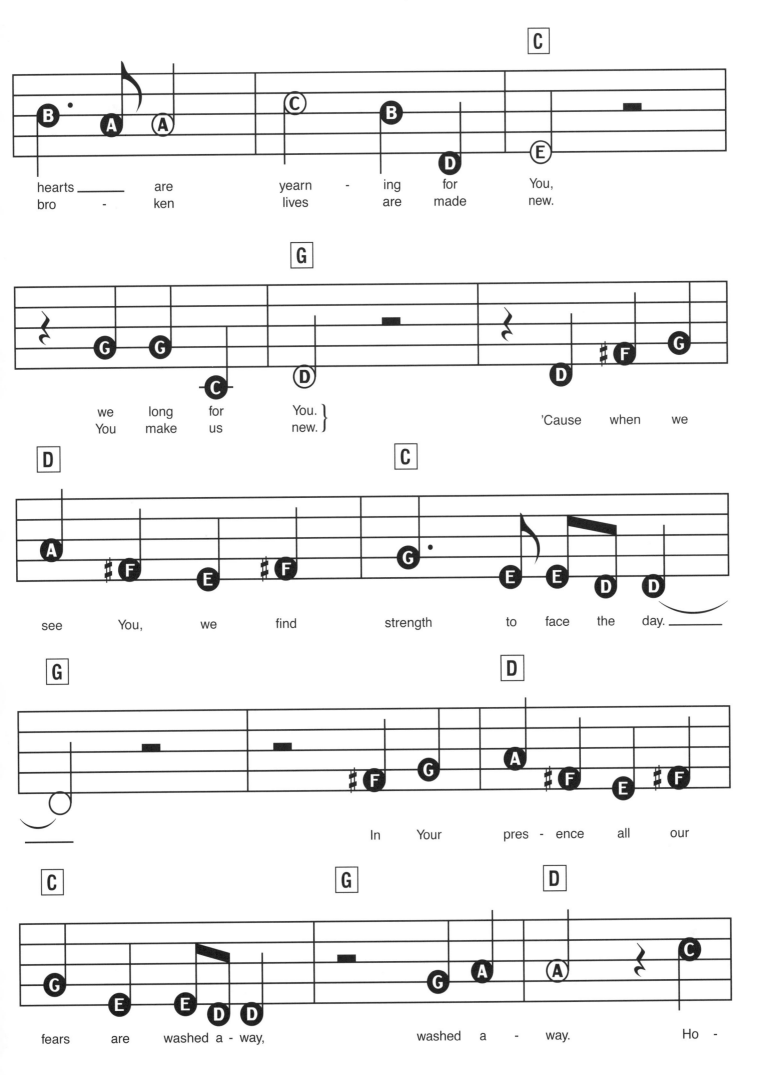

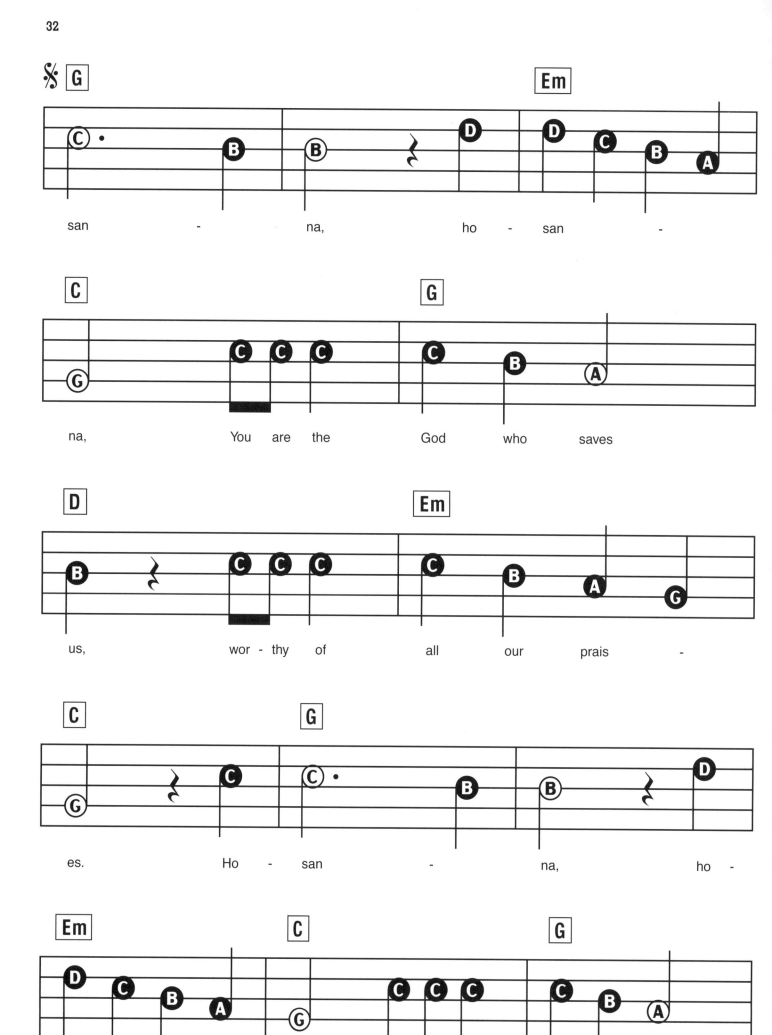

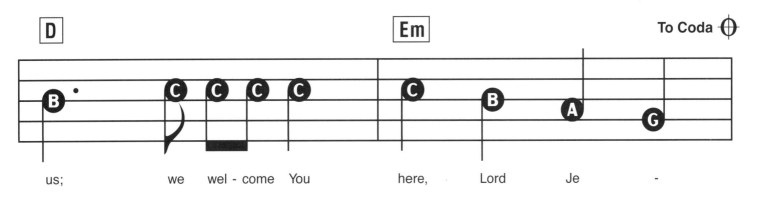

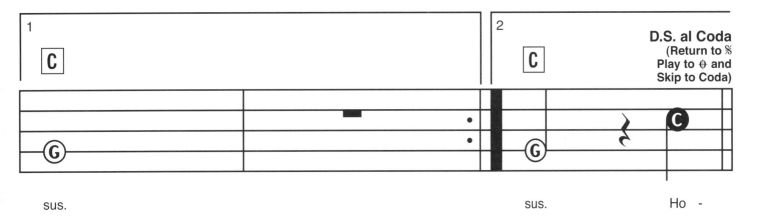

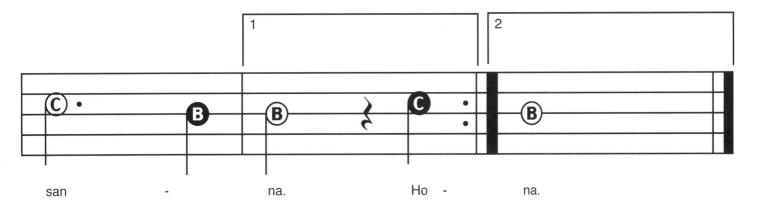

I Am Free

Registration 4
Rhythm: Rock or Pop

Words and Music by
Jon Egan

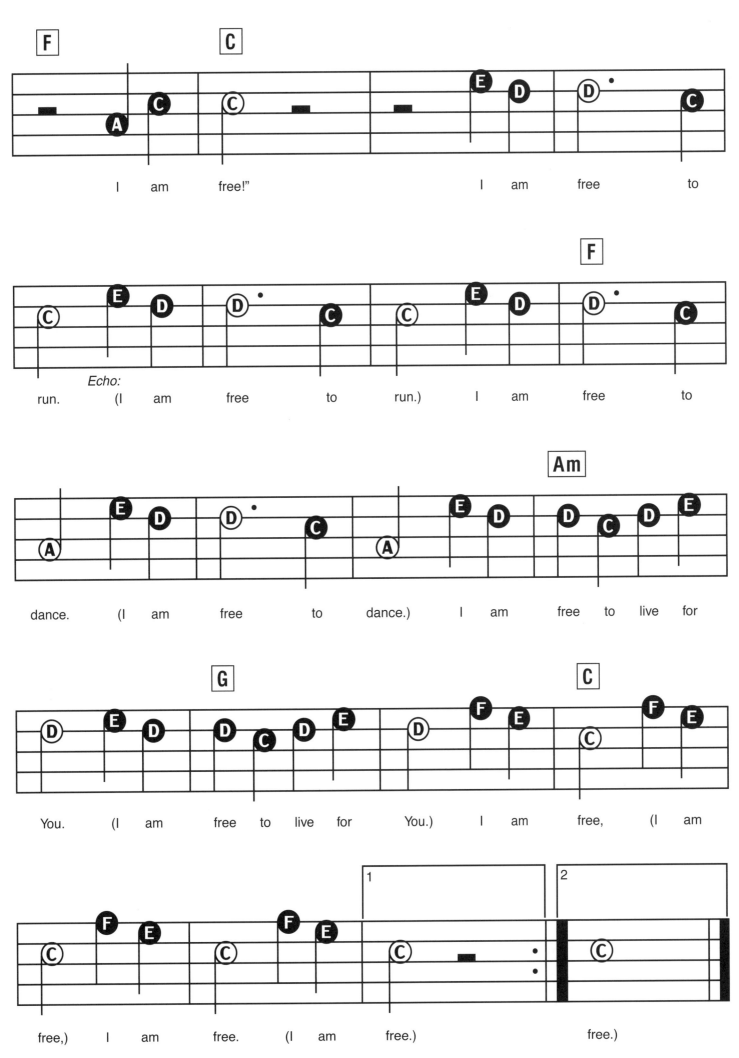

I Will Rise

Registration 8
Rhythm: Ballad or Pop

Words and Music by Chris Tomlin,
Jesse Reeves, Louie Giglio
and Matt Maher

N.C. Em C

There's a | peace I've come to know, | though my
| day that's draw - ing | near | when this

G D Em

heart and flesh may | fail. | There's an | an - chor for my
dark - ness breaks to | light, | and the | shad - ows dis - ap -

C G D

soul. | I can say, | "It is | well."
pear, | and my | faith shall be | my eyes.

G D

Je - sus has o - ver - come, | and the

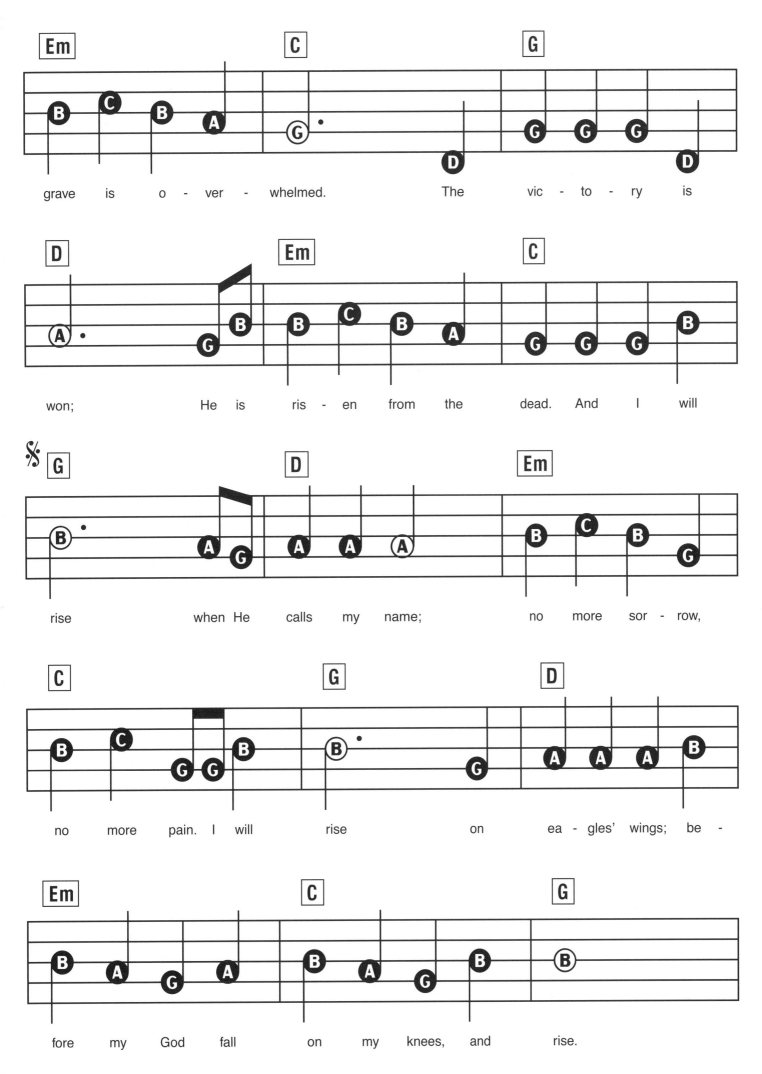

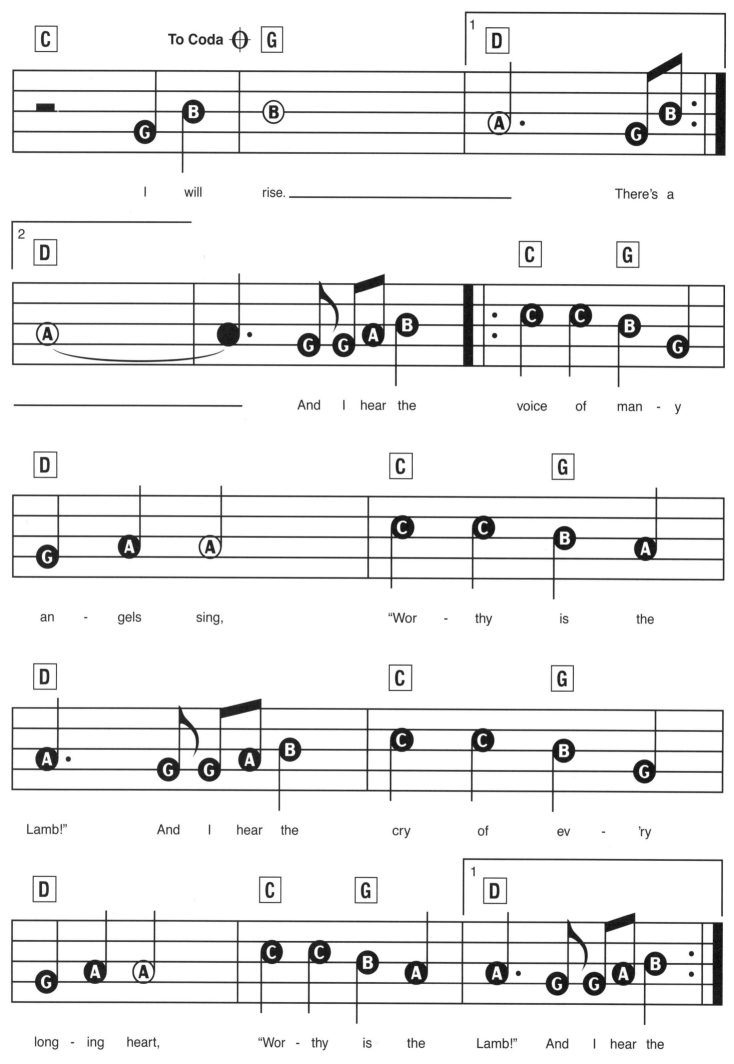

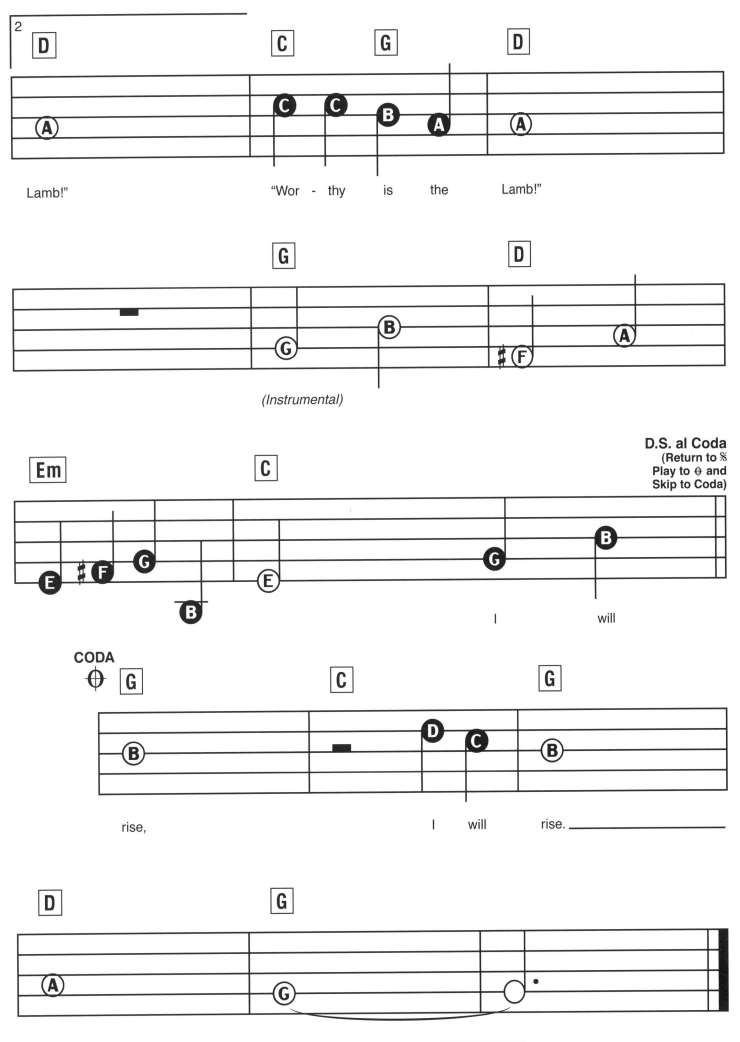

Lord, You Have My Heart

Registration 1
Rhythm: Ballad

Words and Music by
Martin Smith

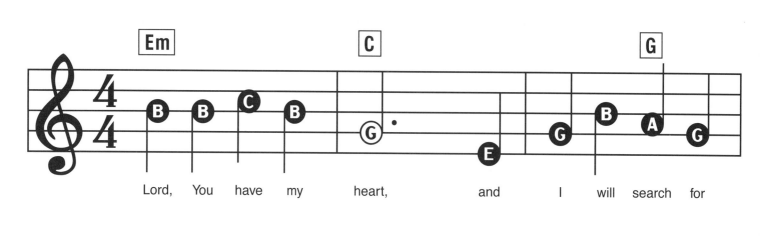

Lord, You have my heart, and I will search for

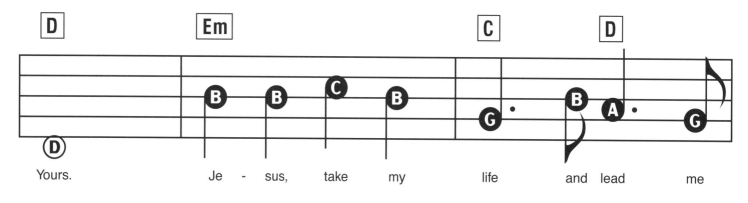

Yours. Je - sus, take my life and lead me

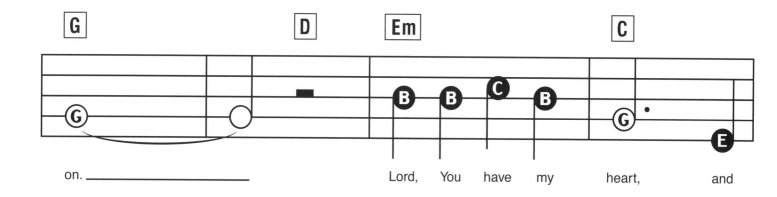

on. _____ Lord, You have my heart, and

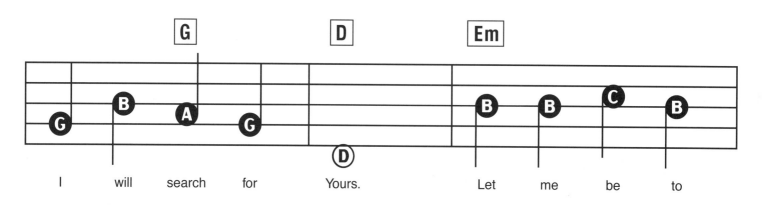

I will search for Yours. Let me be to

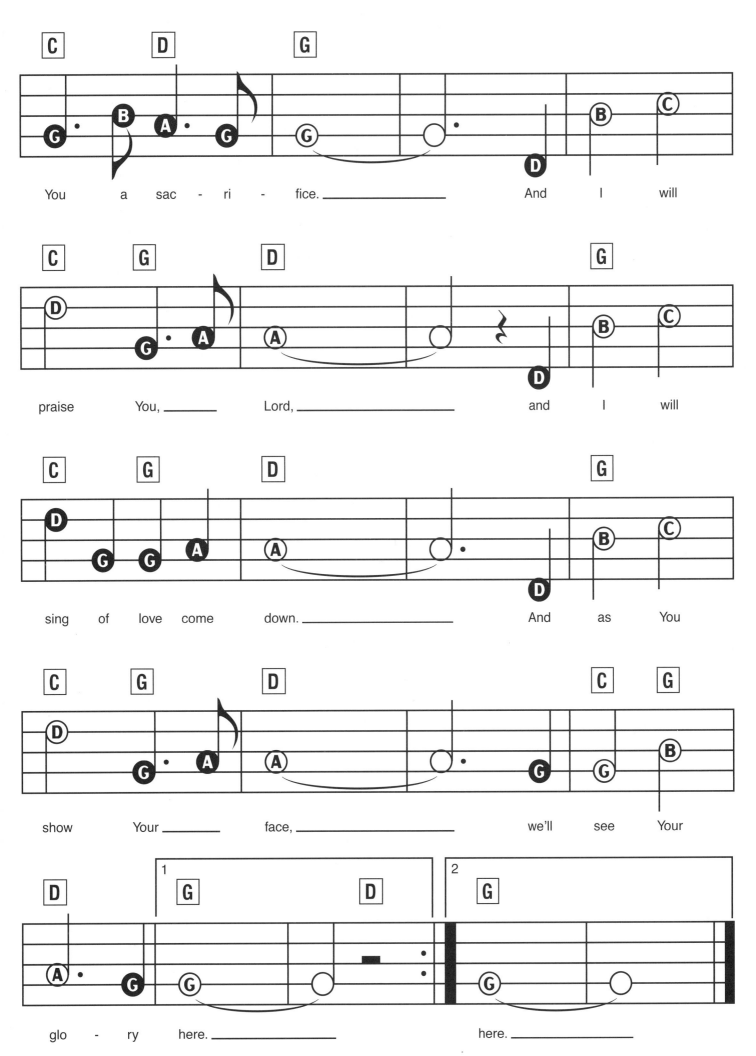

Love the Lord

Registration 4
Rhythm: 16-Beat or Rock

Words and Music by
Lincoln Brewster

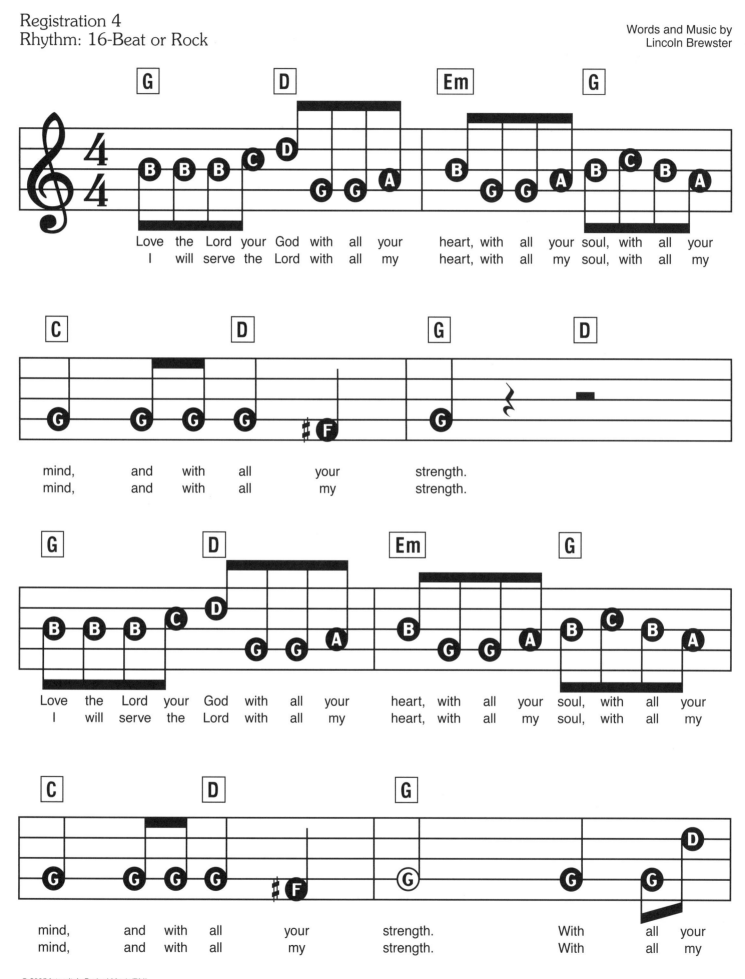

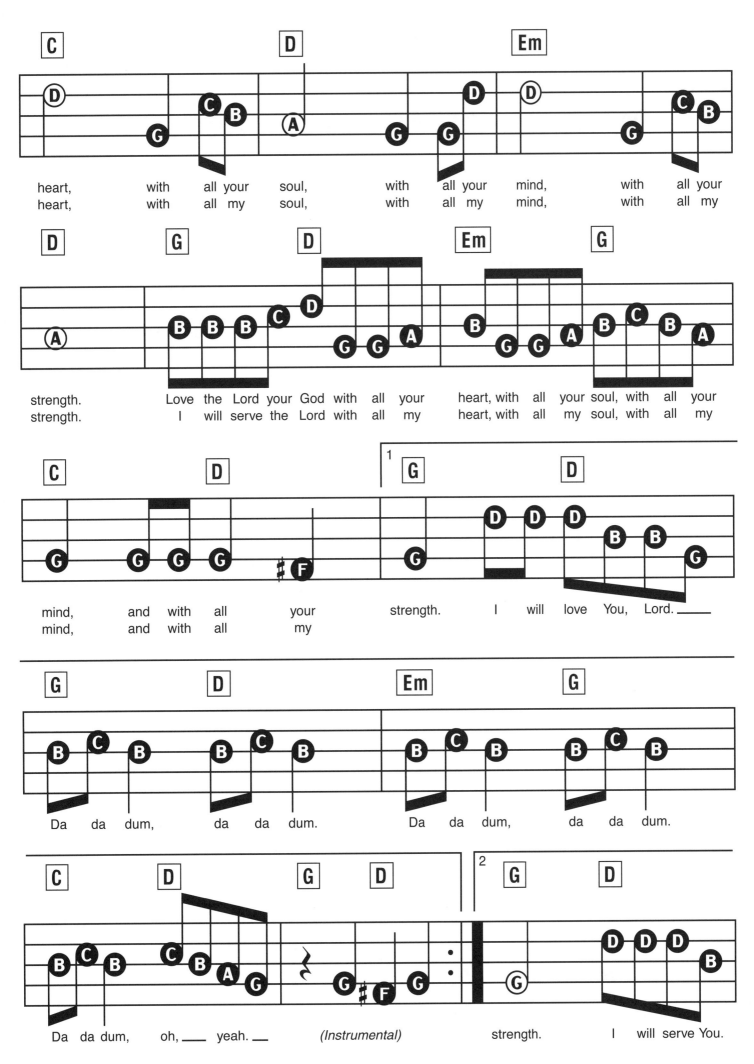

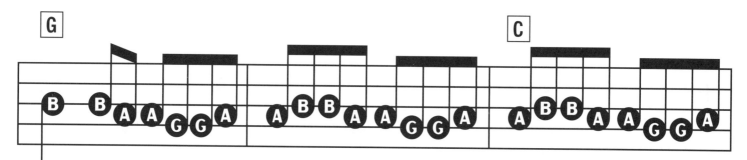

(Instrumental)

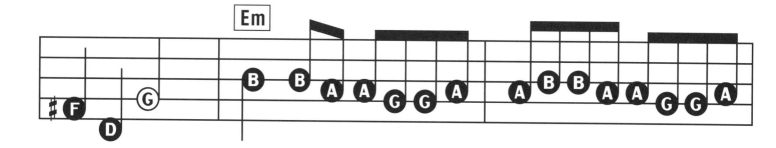

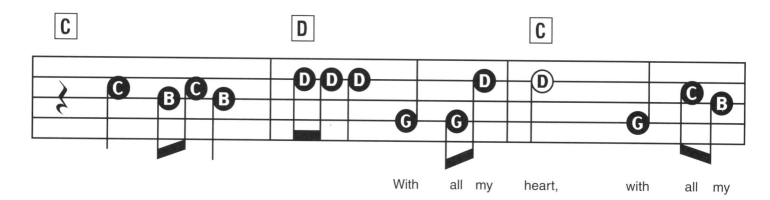

With all my heart, with all my

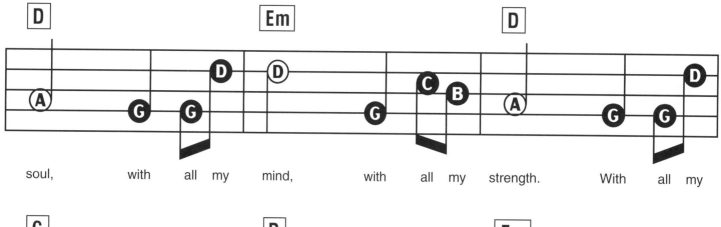

soul, with all my mind, with all my strength. With all my

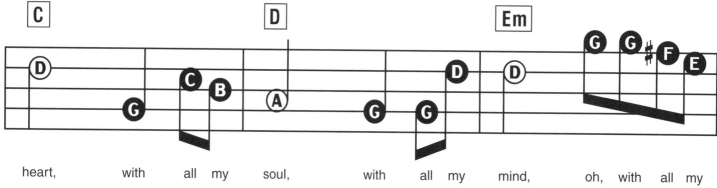

heart, with all my soul, with all my mind, oh, with all my

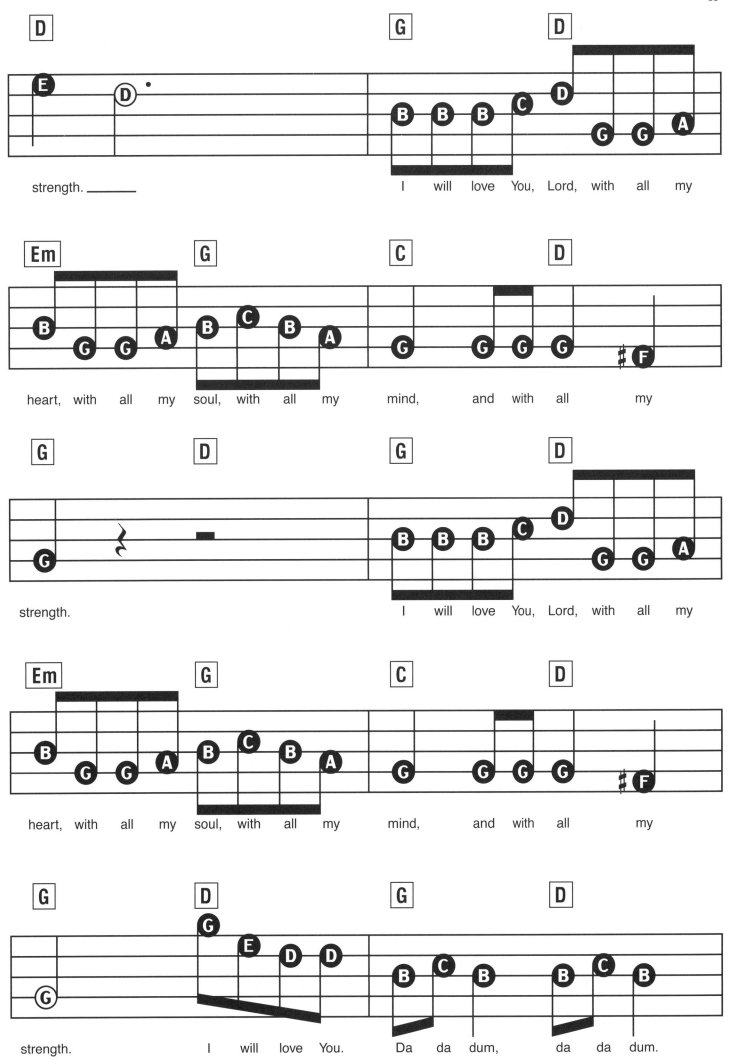

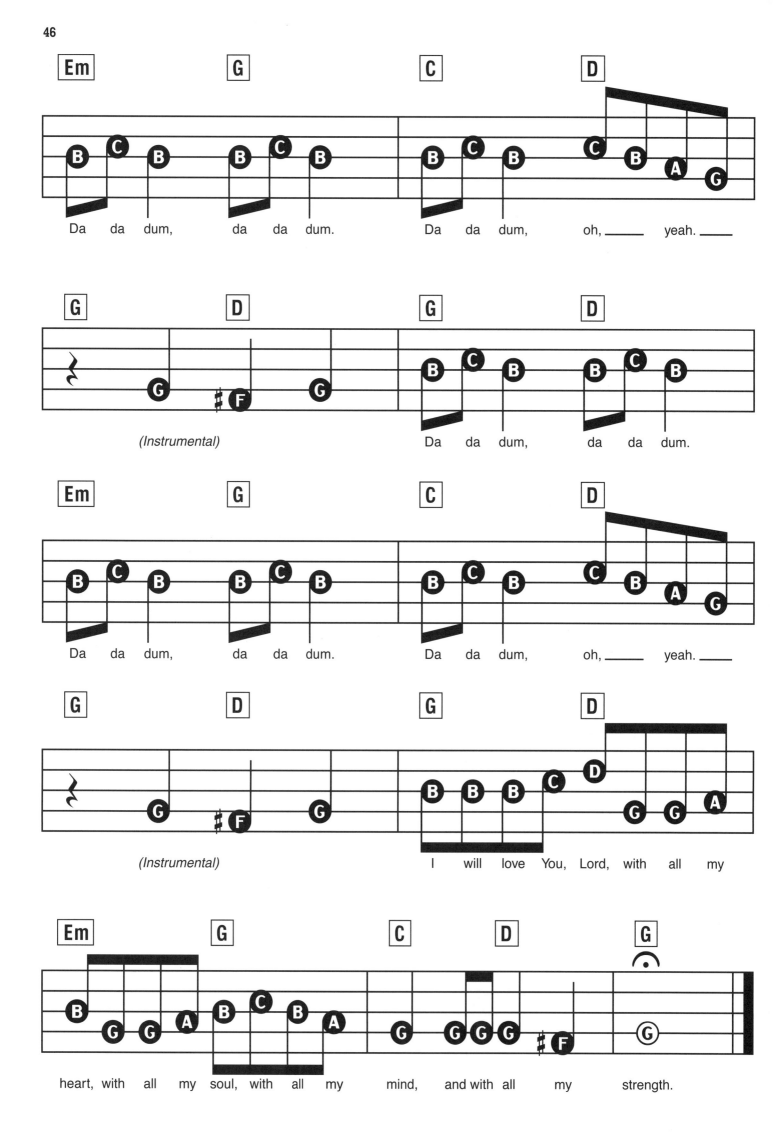

Open the Eyes of My Heart

Registration 8
Rhythm: 8-Beat or Rock

Words and Music by
Paul Baloche

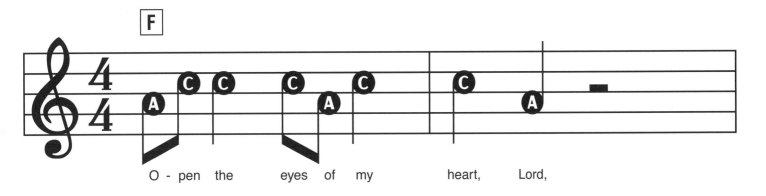

O - pen the eyes of my heart, Lord,

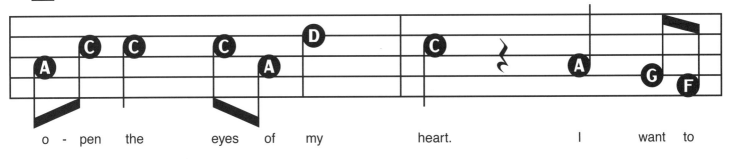

o - pen the eyes of my heart. I want to

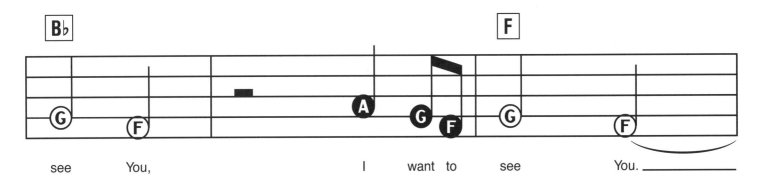

see You, I want to see You. _____

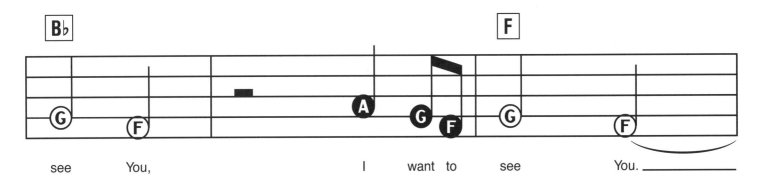

_____ O - pen the eyes of my

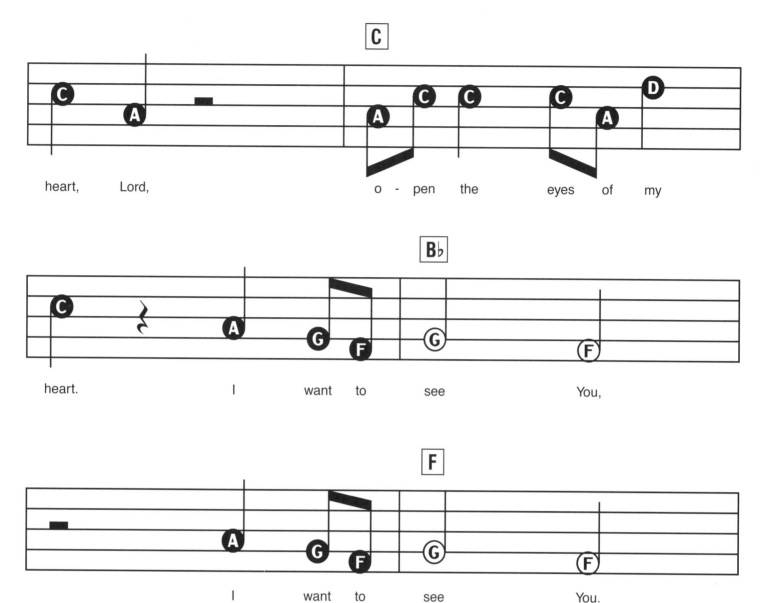

heart,   Lord,   o - pen the   eyes of my

heart.   I   want to   see   You,

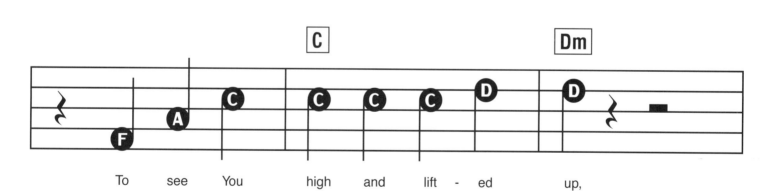

I   want to   see   You.

To see You   high and lift - ed   up,

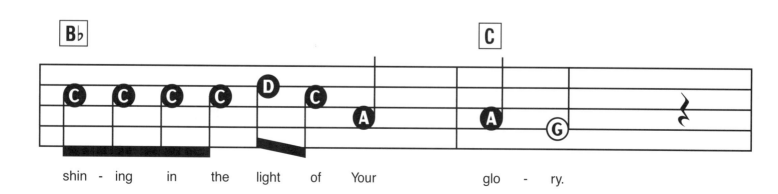

shin - ing in the light of Your   glo - ry.

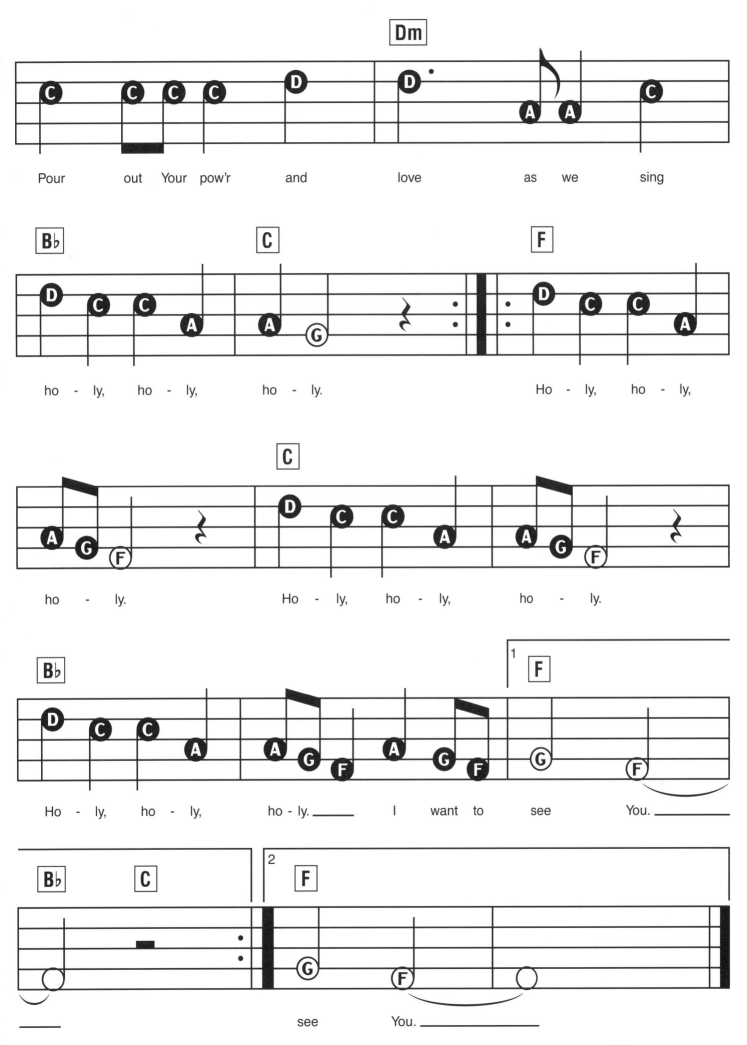

Mighty to Save

Registration 2
Rhythm: Pop or 16-Beat

Words and Music by Ben Fielding
and Reuben Morgan

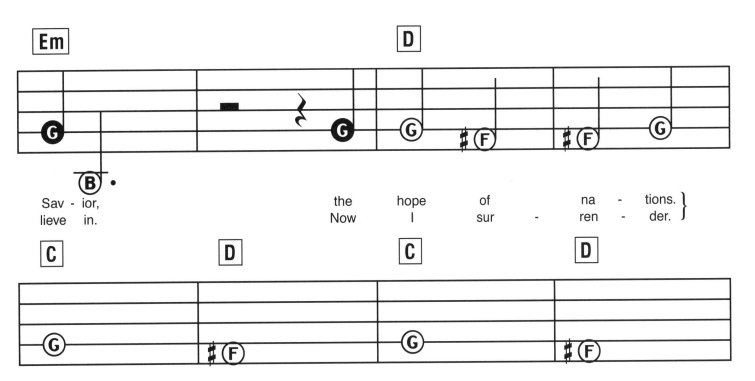

Sav - ior,   the   hope   of   na - tions.
lieve in.   Now   I   sur - ren - der.

(Instrumental)

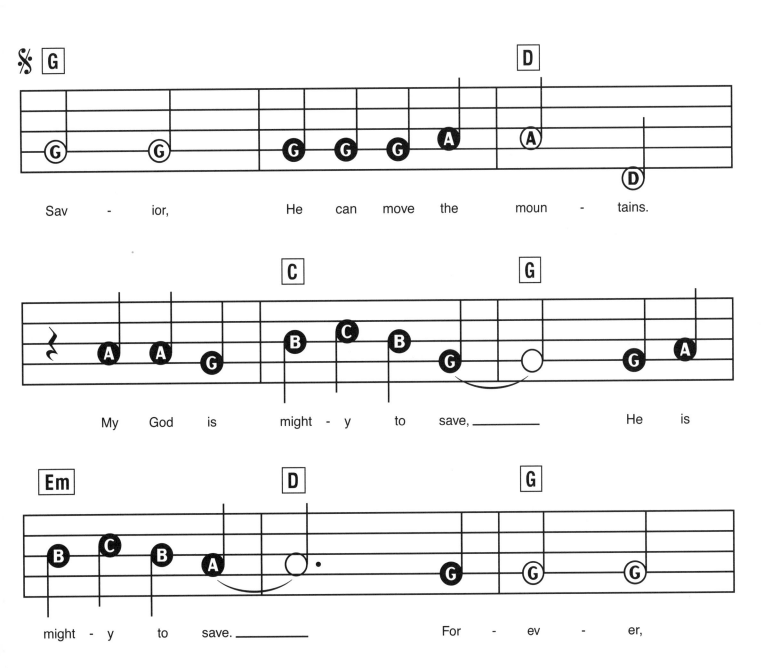

Sav - ior,   He   can   move   the   moun - tains.

My   God   is   might - y   to   save, _____   He   is

might - y   to   save. _____   For - ev - er,

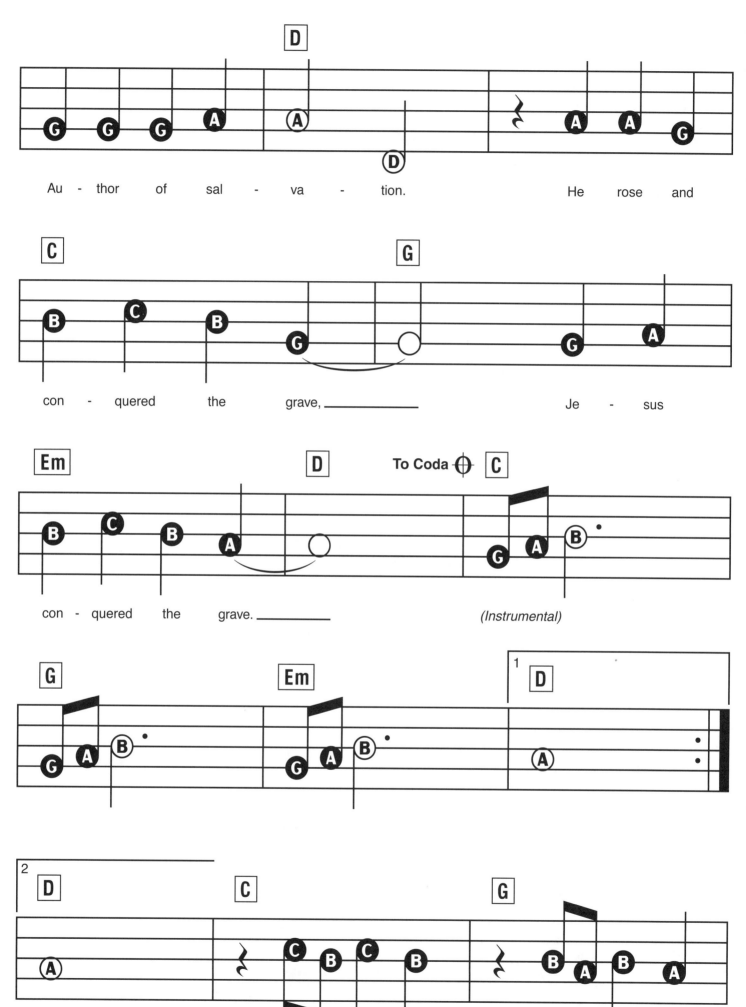

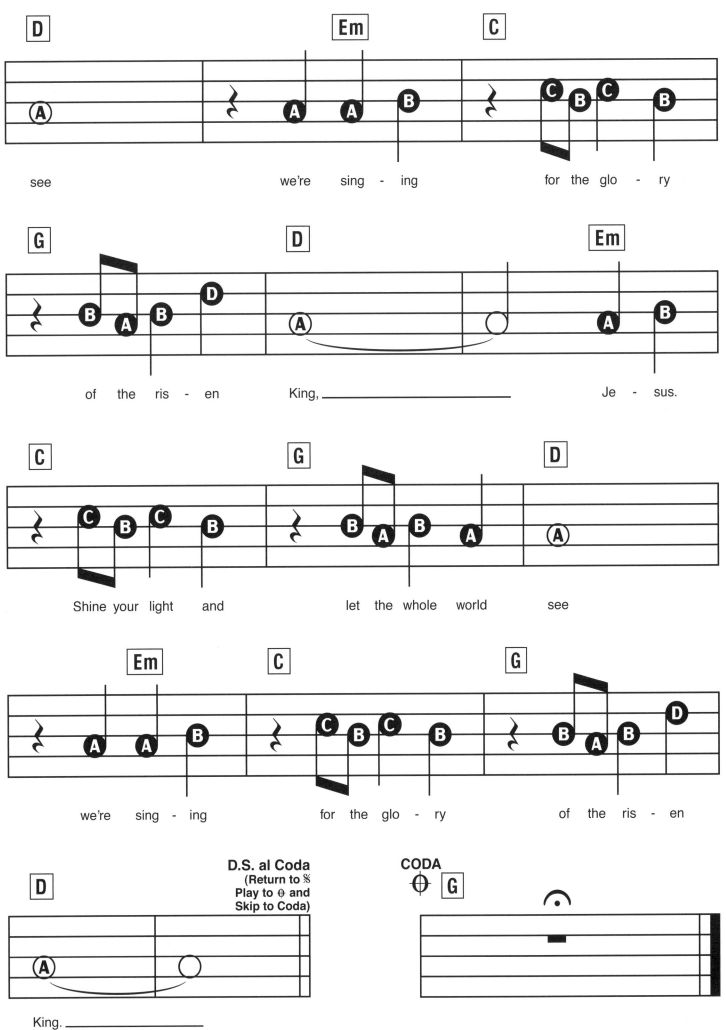

Sing to the King

Registration 4
Rhythm: 16-Beat or Rock

Words and Music by
Billy James Foote

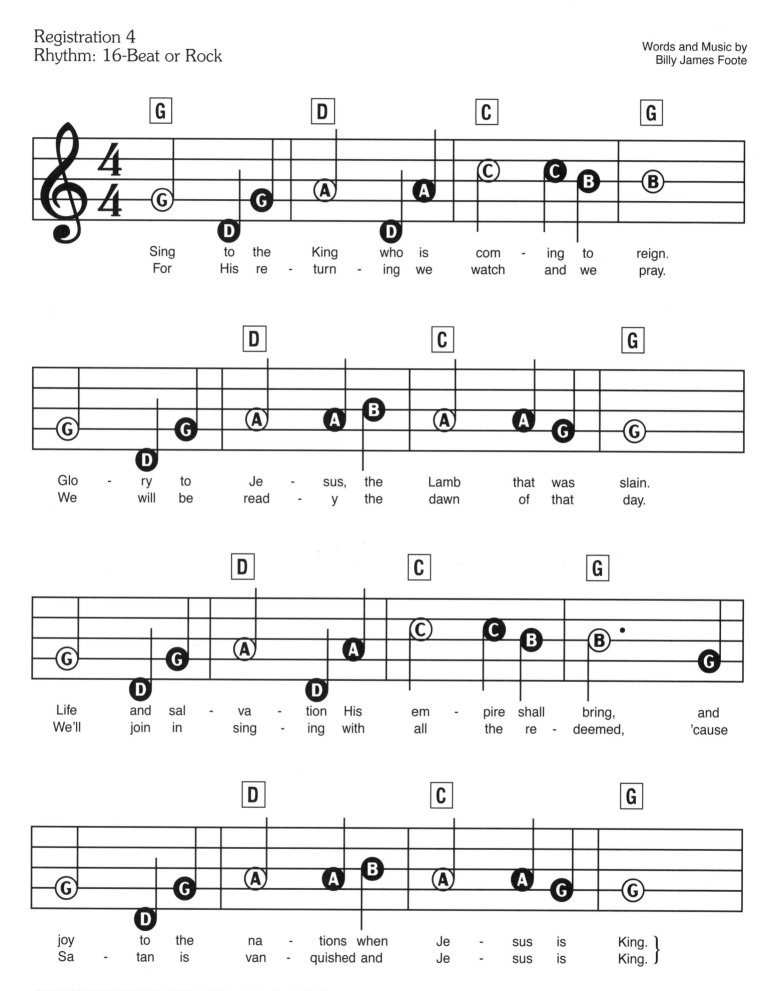

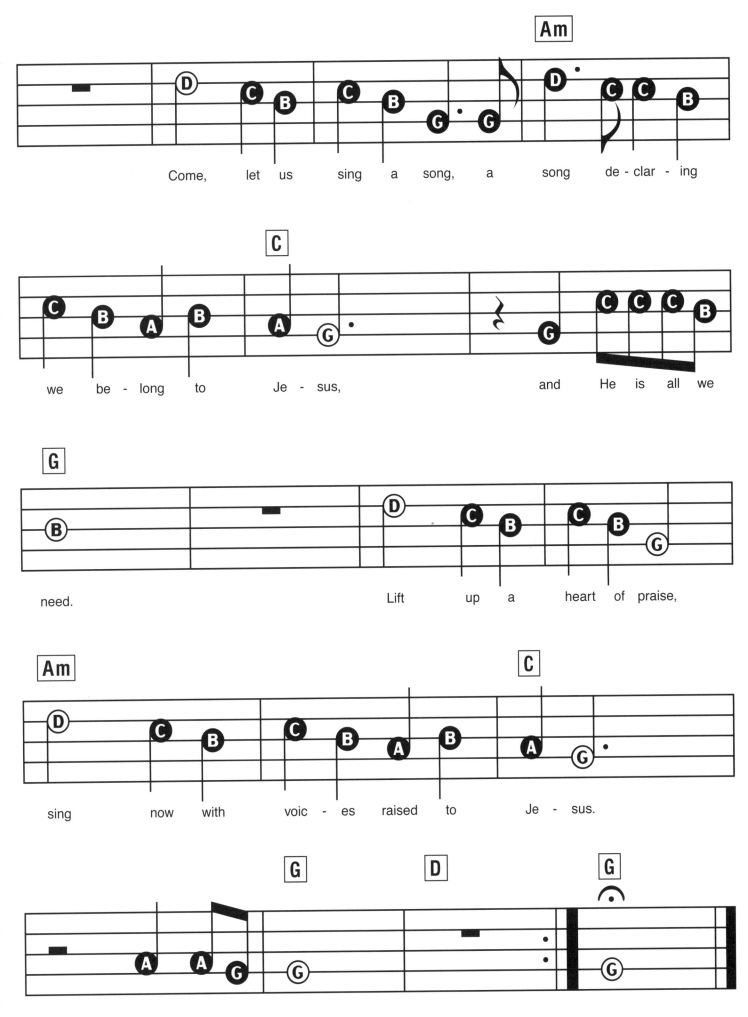

Your Name

Registration 8
Rhythm: Ballad or Pop

Words and Music by Paul Baloche
and Glenn Packiam

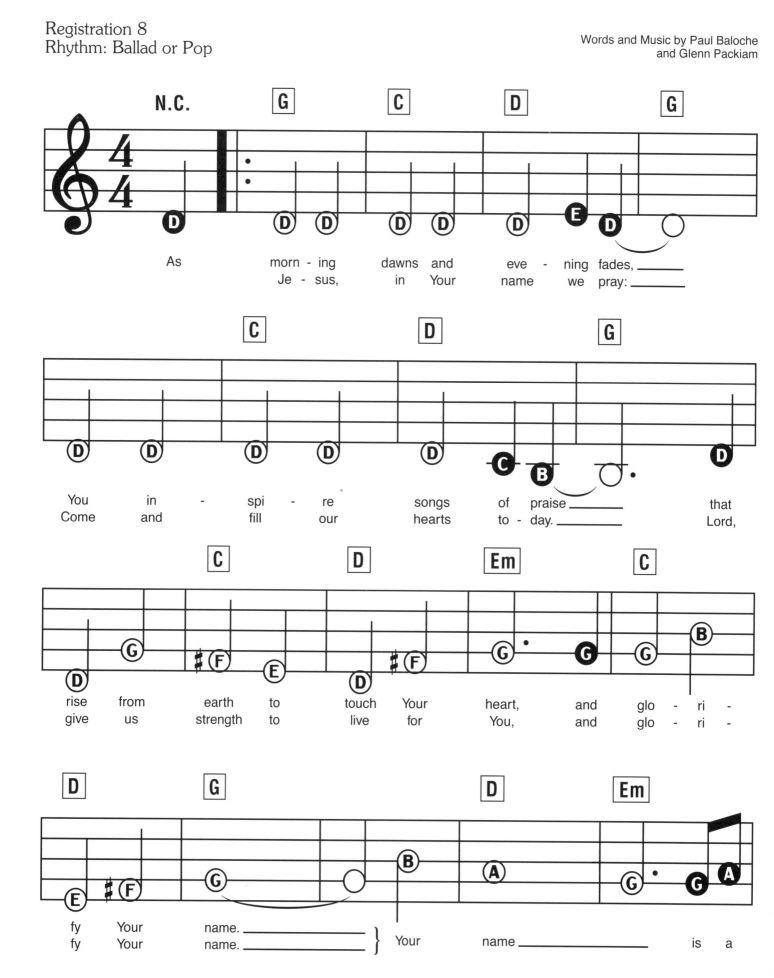

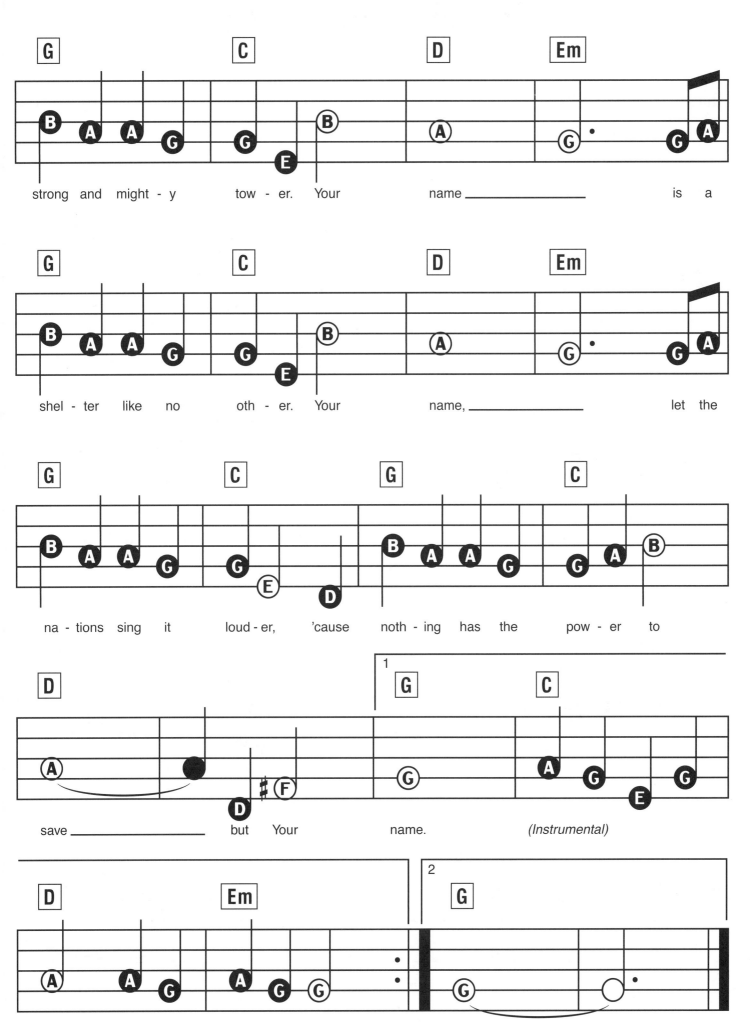

Revelation Song

Registration 8
Rhythm: Ballad or 8-Beat

Words and Music by
Jennie Lee Riddle

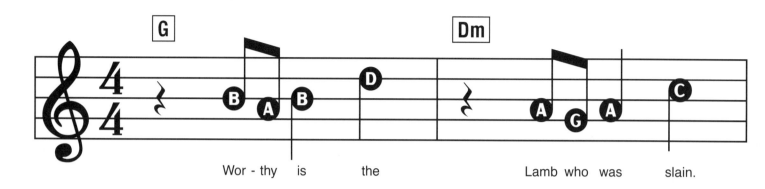

Wor - thy is the Lamb who was slain.

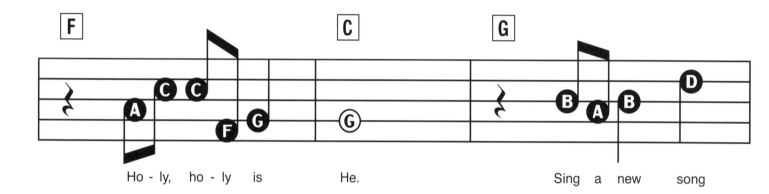

Ho - ly, ho - ly is He. Sing a new song

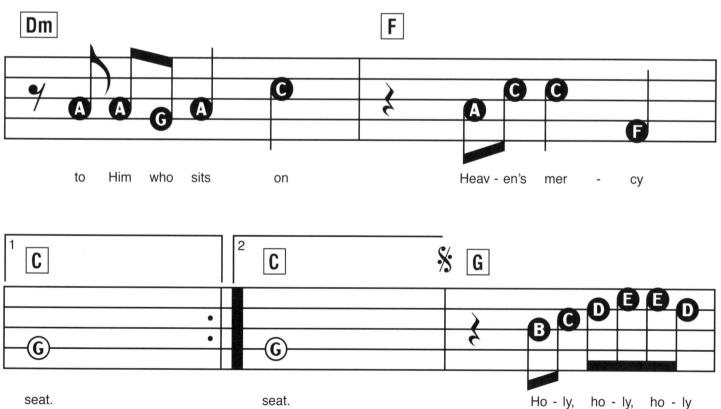

to Him who sits on Heav - en's mer - cy

seat. seat. Ho - ly, ho - ly, ho - ly

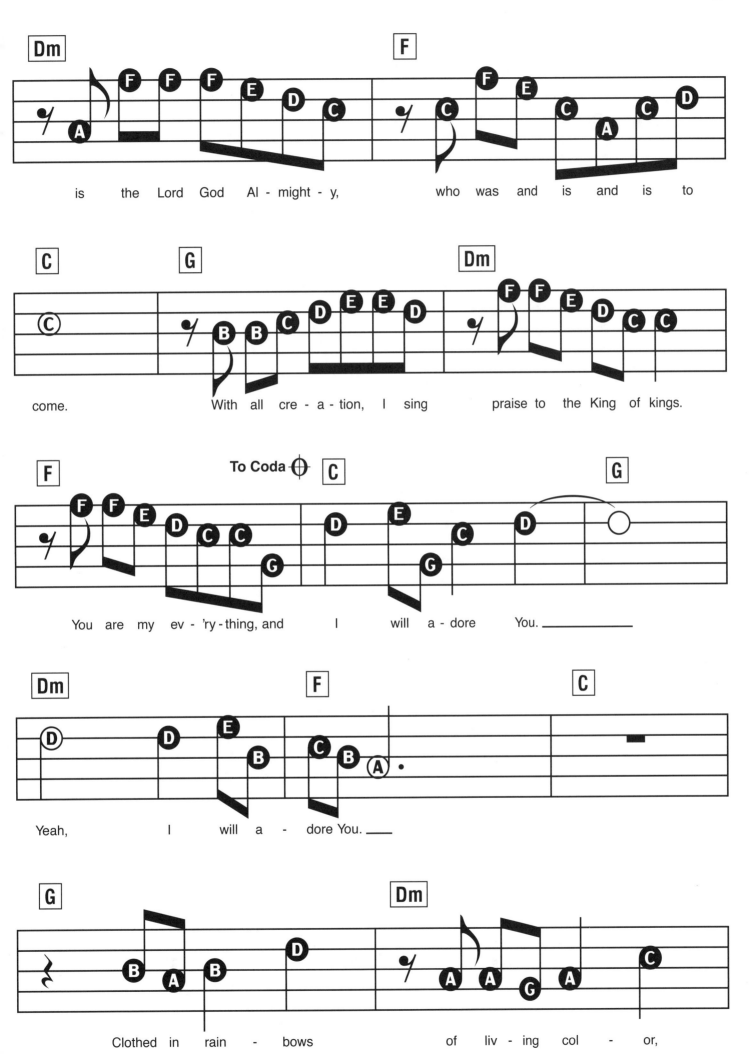

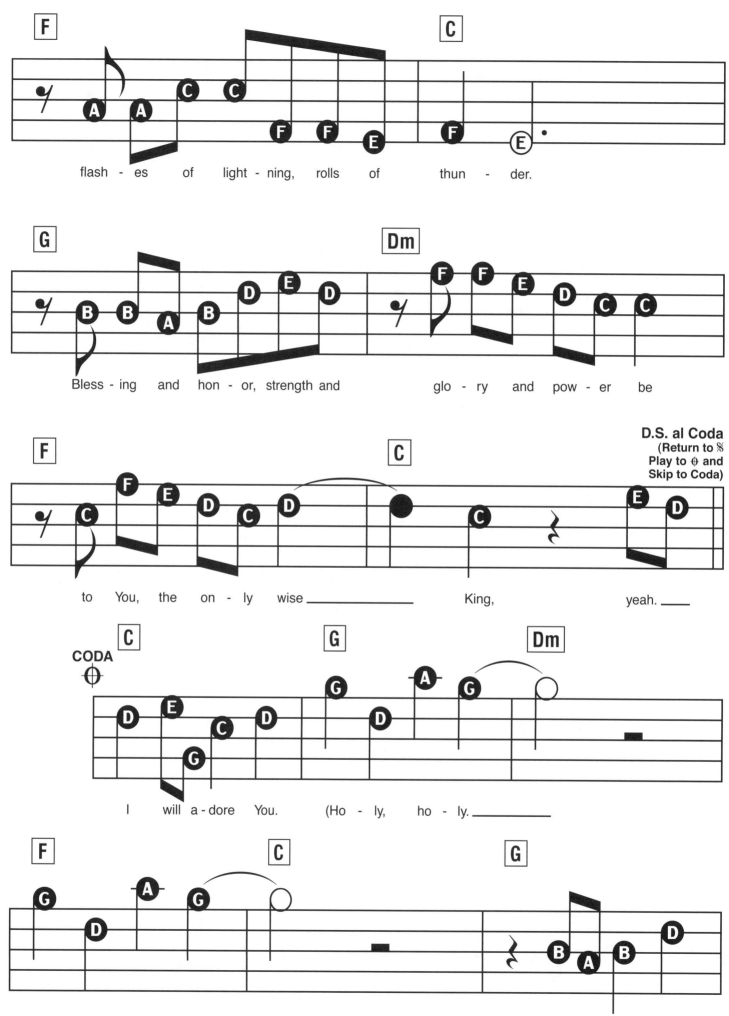

D.S. al Coda
(Return to %
Play to ⊕ and
Skip to Coda)

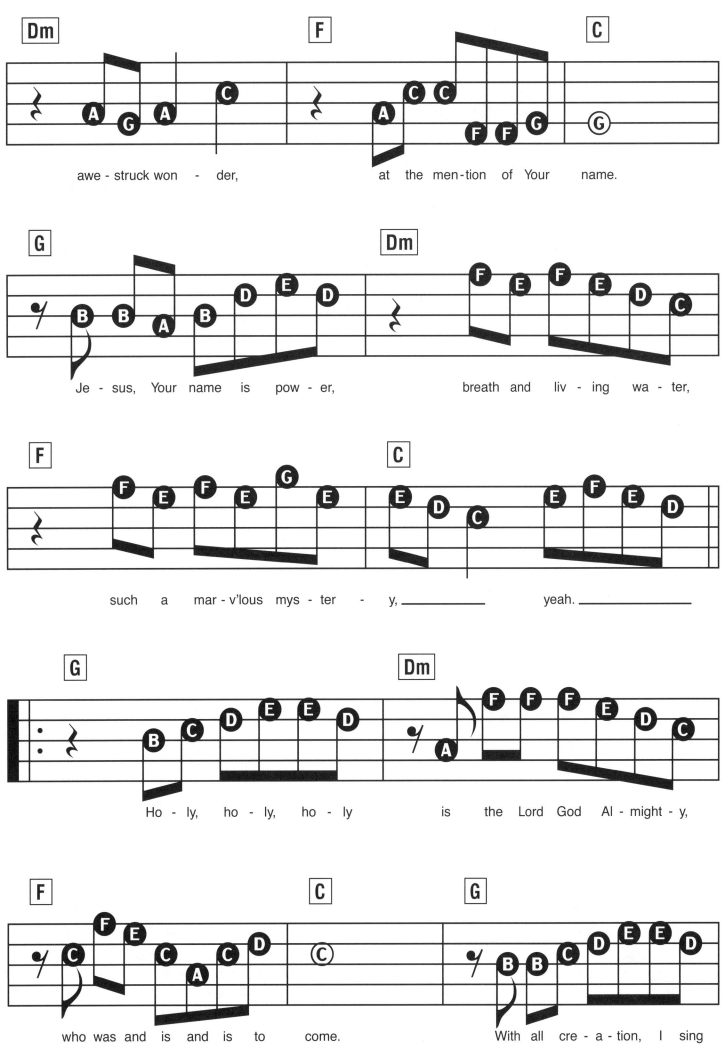

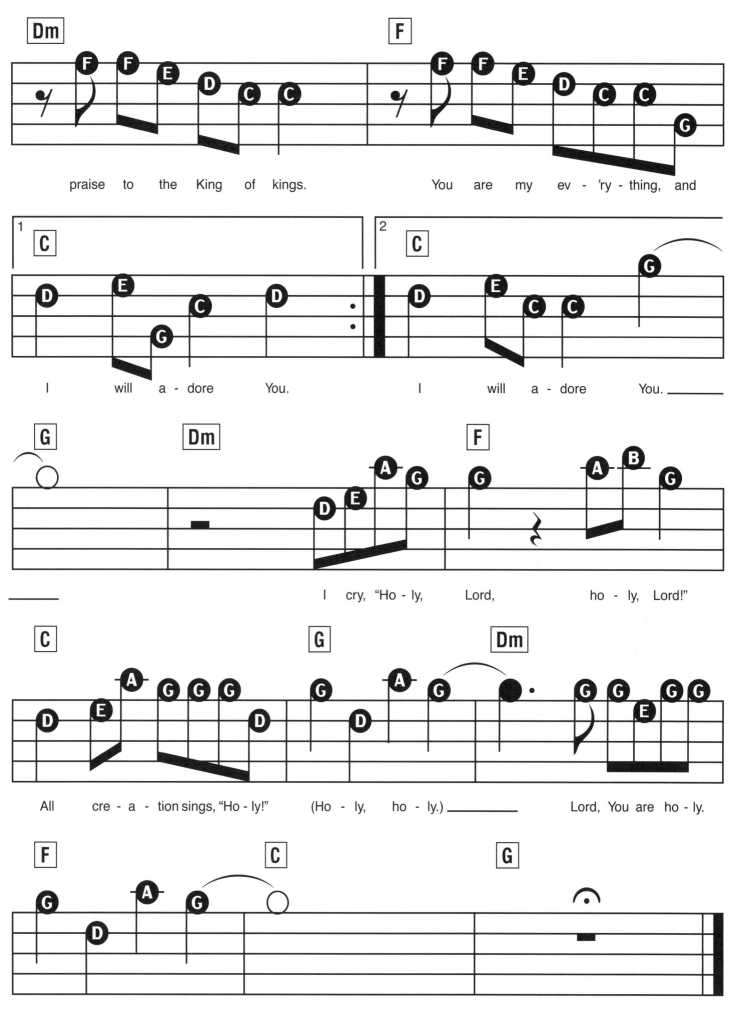

praise to the King of kings.   You are my ev - 'ry - thing, and

I will a - dore You.   I will a - dore You. _____

_____ I cry, "Ho - ly, Lord, ho - ly, Lord!"

All cre - a - tion sings, "Ho - ly!" (Ho - ly, ho - ly.) _____ Lord, You are ho - ly.

(You are ho - ly.) _____

Registration Guide

- Match the Registration number on the song to the corresponding numbered category below. Select and activate an instrumental sound available on your instrument.

- Choose an automatic rhythm appropriate to the mood and style of the song. (Consult your Owner's Guide for proper operation of automatic rhythm features.)

- Adjust the tempo and volume controls to comfortable settings.

Registration

1	Mellow	Flutes, Clarinet, Oboe, Flugel Horn, Trombone, French Horn, Organ Flutes
2	Ensemble	Brass Section, Sax Section, Wind Ensemble, Full Organ, Theater Organ
3	Strings	Violin, Viola, Cello, Fiddle, String Ensemble, Pizzicato, Organ Strings
4	Guitars	Acoustic/Electric Guitars, Banjo, Mandolin, Dulcimer, Ukulele, Hawaiian Guitar
5	Mallets	Vibraphone, Marimba, Xylophone, Steel Drums, Bells, Celesta, Chimes
6	Liturgical	Pipe Organ, Hand Bells, Vocal Ensemble, Choir, Organ Flutes
7	Bright	Saxophones, Trumpet, Mute Trumpet, Synth Leads, Jazz/Gospel Organs
8	Piano	Piano, Electric Piano, Honky Tonk Piano, Harpsichord, Clavi
9	Novelty	Melodic Percussion, Wah Trumpet, Synth, Whistle, Kazoo, Perc. Organ
10	Bellows	Accordion, French Accordion, Mussette, Harmonica, Pump Organ, Bagpipes